Cleopatra Rules!

CLEOPATRA RULES!

THE AMAZING LIFE OF THE ORIGINAL TEEN QUEEN

VICKY ALVEAR SHECTER

BOYDS MILLS PRESS
HONESDALE, PENNSYLVANIA

For my family

The author offers a special thanks to Katrina Dickson, PhD, Department of Classics, Emory University, for her immense help in the initial reading of this book. The author is also extremely grateful to Okasha El Daly, PhD, Egyptologist and director of projects, Foundation for Science, Technology and Civilisation, London; and Dorothy L. King, PhD, archaeologist and military historian, London, for reviewing the manuscript and sharing their knowledge of ancient Egypt and Rome. Tremendous thanks also to Prudence Jones, PhD, of Montclair State University, who reviwed the book contents in proof form. The professional generosity of these experts is both impressive and humbling. Finally, thanks to Mary Harrsch, who generously provided guidance on photo research.

Text copyright © 2010

Boyds Mills Press, Inc.
815 Church Street
Honesdale, Pennsylvania 18431
Printed in the United States of America

Library of Congress Cataloging-in-Publication Data

Shecter, Vicky.
  Cleopatra rules! : the amazing life of the original teen queen / Vicky Alvear Shecter. — 1st ed.
    p. cm.
  Includes bibliographical references and index.
  ISBN 978-1-59078-718-2 (hardcover : alk. paper)
  1. Cleopatra, Queen of Egypt, d. 30 B.C.—Juvenile literature. 2. Queens—Egypt—Biography—Juvenile literature. 3. Egypt—History—332-30 B.C.—Juvenile literature. I. Title.
  DT92.7.S54 2010
  932'.021092—dc22
  [B]
                              2009026737

First edition
The text of this book is set in 13-point Berkeley Oldstyle Book.

10 9 8 7 6 5 4 3 2 1

Contents

Introduction

Actress Lilly Langtry (1853–1929) as Cleopatra.

WAS THE LAST QUEEN OF EGYPT
an evil, gorgeous woman, dripping with jewels? A power-hungry temptress trying to rule the world? A pharaoh with a small snake problem?

How about none of the above.

7

Everything you've read about Queen Cleopatra VII should have come with a warning: *details may have been "Photoshopped" and manipulated beyond recognition.* The Queen of the Nile had more mud flung at her than you can dig up on the banks of that great river. From Shakespeare to Hollywood, what you've seen and read about her wasn't always completely true.

Hollywood made her into a hot starlet because nobody wanted to see an ugly queen. Historians turned her into a power-hungry witch because that made her story more interesting. And her Roman conqueror, Octavian, made her into a weapon of mass destruction in heels so he could stomp all over Mark Antony.

Will we ever know the real Cleopatra? Without her personal letters and journals, probably not. But for the first time, modern scholars and historians are looking at events from the queen's point of view. What they are finding is that Queen Cleopatra VII, the last pharaoh of Egypt, was in fact a brilliant, complex, powerful ruler. For twenty years, she kept the world's greatest superpower from taking over her country—a good trick when you realize it was during the time when Rome swallowed up countries faster than most teens use up text minutes.

How did she do it?

The answer may shock and surprise you—and may even make you laugh. Either way, you'll get a more balanced look at Cleopatra the queen, the ruler, and mother of four. So, on your knees, commoner. The last great queen of Egypt is about to take the stage!

1

A Bookish Nerd?

Who knew? The queen, famous for her infamous relationships, started out caring more about books than boys.

SHE RULED ALL OF EGYPT, had Romans trembling in their togas, and made kings weak at the knees. Yet the glamour queen of the ancient world started out as … a bookish nerd.

Yup, the girl whom Shakespeare likened to Venus—the goddess of love—cared more about books than boys. At first, anyway. As a kid, Cleopatra spent most of her time hitting the scrolls at the famous Great Library of Alexandria.

Young Cleopatra had a good reason for being so serious—several reasons, actually: her ambitious brothers and sisters. Life with them was like living with a nest of squirming, hissing reality-show stars—you never knew when one might strike. Would her older sister push Cleopatra down the palace steps to get her out of the way? Would her younger brothers and sister poison her afternoon snack? Or maybe, "accidentally on purpose," hold her head under the water a little too long while they played in the palace pool?

See, Cleopatra's family was not what you would exactly call … um, loving. Yet while most of her family members cared only for their own personal power, Cleopatra longed to bring back the glory days of her beloved country, which was easier said than done.

Corrupt rulers and a long history of border disputes had weakened the once powerful kingdom. By the time Cleopatra came along, Egypt was sliding down the tubes faster than a greased-up preschooler on a Slip 'n Slide.

Turning to the Big Bad Wolf

As Egypt declined, Pharaoh Ptolemy XII took his eleven-year-old daughter, Cleopatra VII, on a trip to Rome—not to sightsee but to save his skin. Raging mobs had run him off his throne and out of Alexandria. See, over the years, Daddy Pharaoh had paid Roman generals big bucks in return for soldiers to scare off his enemies. Only he had so many enemies, he had to buy more Roman protection. And guess who footed the bill—Egyptian citizens, who had to pay extra taxes. When Cleopatra's dad taxed his people to the breaking point to pay for more Roman henchmen, they chased him out of Alexandria faster than a band of crazed shoppers at a half-off sale.

But although the pharaoh may have been out, he wasn't down. Not

 10

without a fight, anyway. So he put his kingdom into even deeper debt—this time to a private Roman loan shark—to pay Roman armies for help in invading his own country. Yes, that's right, *he invaded his own country*. It worked. The Roman military put him back in charge. But as a result, his people hated him more than ever.

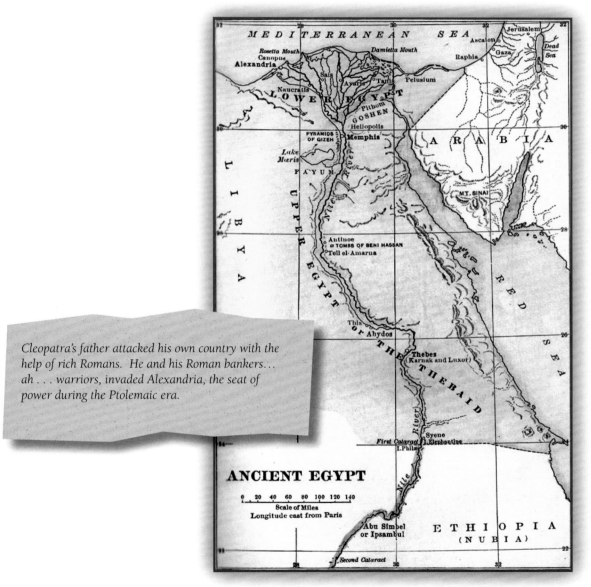

Cleopatra's father attacked his own country with the help of rich Romans. He and his Roman bankers… ah . . . warriors, invaded Alexandria, the seat of power during the Ptolemaic era.

ANCIENT EGYPT

0 20 40 60 80 100 120 140
Scale of Miles
Longitude east from Paris

"Who You Calling Fatty?"

Most rulers want nicknames that reflect their power or glory, like Alexander the Great or William the Conqueror.

Cleopatra's dad? He ended up with a nickname that probably made her cringe. The people called him Auletes (owl-ee-tees)—the Piper—because Ptolemy (*tall*-oh-mee) XII liked to play the flute. They didn't call him the Piper in a nice way, either. Guys who played wind instruments in the ancient world weren't exactly considered macho.

Still, it was better than her grandfather's nickname. They called him Chickpea. Before that, the Egyptians called Cleopatra's great-grandfather—Ptolemy VIII—Fatty, or Physcon (*fiss*-con), because of his huge size. He needed several servants to hold him up to waddle around the palace!

Whatever she thought about these nicknames, Cleopatra likely had a bigger issue with the way her father groveled at the feet of rich Romans.

Like her dad, she knew the Egyptians needed Rome to survive. But unlike him, she was determined to find a way to become Rome's partner, instead of its slave.

While the Piper and Cleopatra trolled for money in Rome, his oldest daughter, Berenice, snatched the throne and named herself queen. Okay, we know Cleopatra was smart, but could her sister have been any dumber?

Think about it: most usurpers (people who steal thrones) usually have the king killed *before* they name themselves top dog. Yet for some reason, Berenice didn't. That's why some scholars wonder if maybe somebody else shoved her on the throne while Daddy was on the road. Or whether she thought Daddy would be assassinated in Rome. Or even thought that angry mobs in Egypt would tear him apart once they heard how much they would owe in taxes to pay the Roman loan shark.

Either way, it was a dumb move, because as soon as Daddy regained control of the throne, Berenice parted with more than her crown. She parted with her life, too. The Piper had her pipes cut—she was executed for treason. Turns out that Daddy the Flute Player could turn into Daddy the Destroyer without pausing for breath.

Cleopatra took careful note of that move, too.

Cleopatra's father taxed his people to the breaking point in order to pay back the Romans. And what they wanted to break was him!

Most of what we know about Cleopatra comes from the Romanized Greek historian Plutarch, who wrote about Mark Antony nearly one hundred years after Cleopatra's death.

Plutarch needed to make Mark Antony—and therefore Cleopatra—look bad because he did not want to anger the often touchy Roman emperor(s) of his time.

Imagine if Lex Luthor wrote Superman's bio or Darth Vader dished on Princess Leia. You might find yourself a little skeptical about their claims, right? You might even find yourself doubting—if not laughing outright at—all of the insults and snide remarks.

Yet that's exactly what happened to Cleopatra. Rome won, so Romans told their version of her story. The Romans dissed and dismissed her worse than a fashion critic at the Oscars.

Today's scholars are not so quick to accept everything the Romans wrote about Cleopatra. They look for proof—or at least some evidence—that might either back up or dispute the Romans' version of events. More importantly, they do what the Romans found unthinkable: they give her the respect of seeing things from her point of view.

It's about time the great queen received the equal—if not royal—treatment she always deserved.

Cleopatra, like all educated Greeks, would have learned to read using Homer's (right) epic poems, The Iliad and The Odyssey.

After the Piper snuffed his eldest daughter, he retook the throne and went back to playing the flute. Egyptians seethed over having to fork over even more of their hard-earned money in taxes to repay Romans. But what could they do? The streets of Alexandria teemed with Roman soldiers paid to keep the Piper piping and the people quiet.

Meanwhile, young Cleopatra chilled at the Great Library of Alexandria, studying science, mathematics, philosophy, and languages. In fact, according to one ancient source, she was the first ruler in nearly 250 years to learn and speak the native Egyptian language!

Wait. What? How could Egyptian rulers *not* speak the native tongue?

Easy. Cleopatra's family—the Ptolemy line of Pharaohs—wasn't Egyptian. Cleopatra actually descended from the Greeks. Nearly 250 years earlier, Alexander the Great invaded Egypt and put it under his rule. When he died, his general and self-claimed half brother Ptolemy took over as pharaoh. From then on, his Greek descendants ruled Egypt and spoke only Greek. Even Cleopatra's name was Greek.

15

Alexander the Great, a Macedonian Greek, conquered Egypt centuries before Cleopatra. Her ancestor Ptolemy I, Alexander's top general, claimed he and Alexander were half brothers.

It just happened to be the name of Alexander the Great's little sister.

Our Cleo had a talent for languages. In addition to Greek and Egyptian, she spoke numerous African dialects as well as Arabic, Aramaic, Hebrew, Latin, and Persian. But her political smarts were even more impressive. And she couldn't wait to put them to good use.

Teenage Queen on a Tear

The Piper piped his last tune by the time Cleopatra turned seventeen. The good news was that dearly departed Daddy named her queen before he died. The bad news? She had to share the throne with her ten-year-old half brother, Ptolemy XIII, as king. The Piper probably expected the two to marry when the boy got older. And the *ewww!* factor gets even worse. After all, Cleopatra's mother was likely also her aunt, her father's sister. Brother-sister royal marriages were an ancient Egyptian custom. (See story of Isis and Osiris, page 21.)

But that didn't mean Cleopatra *liked* the idea of having to marry her little brother. It's easy to imagine the sounds of her gagging echoing throughout the marble-columned halls of the palace.

The new mini-king could barely keep his sandals tied, so he had a group of power-hungry advisers working for him. They wanted big sis off the throne. And fast. That way, they could rule in the kid's place until he reached adulthood—and maybe even longer if they dug their claws into him deep enough.

Cleopatra knew what they were up to. So she made a gutsy move. Instead of hanging around the palace at Alexandria watching her little brother and his men plot her destruction, she went down the Nile on a little public relations tour of the kingdom to solidify her power base.

It worked. Little bro and his advisers had a cow over being left behind. They probably cried their black kohl (Egyptian eyeliner) off in frustration.

Holy Cow!

Montu, the Egyptian god of war, was sometimes shown with a falcon head, sometimes as a bull; later Montu was associated with the sacred Buchis bull. Cleopatra milked her role in the Buchis ceremony—celebrating Montu—for all it was worth.

On her tour, Cleopatra got word that the sacred Buchis (*boo-kiss*) bull had died. Only one Buchis bull lived at a time. When that one died, another was chosen and made ready to take its place in a huge ceremony. Cleopatra's timing couldn't have been better. She accompanied the replacement bull to its new temple digs near the city of Thebes in Upper Egypt. Then, surrounded by priests and powerful politicians, she led the sacred rites. The crowds went bull-istic.

The Egyptians probably loved the fact that she spoke their native language and honored their ancient practices. It's easy to imagine the young queen dripping power and confidence as she walked with her head held high.

Not bad for a teen queen. But all the loving she got in Upper Egypt only made her more hated back down at the palace.

The Advisers Play While the Queen Is Away

Cleopatra had a reputation for getting the job done. This royal decree bears what most scholars believe is the queen's catch-all catch phrase, the Greek word "Genestho"—which means "Make it happen." That pretty much summed up her personality, don't you think?

While Cleopatra surveyed her kingdom and charmed her public, her little brother's advisers turned on her at home in Alexandria. They pushed an Egyptian law that said if a queen and king ruled together, the king always took first place and the queen second—even if the king was still a kid. They figured they could take control of the kingdom in his name. They did not realize who they were up against.

Cleopatra stayed in command until the worst happened. Drought and crop failures brought famine throughout the land. The king's advisers blamed Cleopatra and manipulated the politicians and crowds.

Taking the Bull by the Horns

How now dead cow? The Egyptians mummified sacred bulls in the hopes that they would continue protecting Egypt in the afterworld.

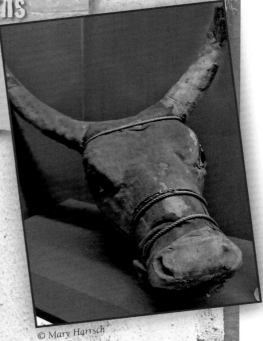

© Mary Harrsch

Cleopatra milked the death of the Buchis bull for all it was worth. She participated in its burial and escorted the replacement bull to its sanctuary in Hermonthis, a city near Thebes. The Buchis bull was believed to be the incarnation of the war god, Montu.

When a Buchis bull died, it was mummified and placed in a special tomb called the Bucheion. A funerary stone marking Cleopatra's participation in the ceremonies calls her "the Queen, the Lady of the Two Lands, the Goddess Philopater." Cleopatra likely impressed the priests and her people with her ability to recite the prayers and lead the rituals in their sacred language.

A Buchis bull was identified by special markings—black face and white body with backward-growing hair. When a new male calf was selected, it lived in the temple, ate the best foods, received offerings, and enjoyed an "udderly" pampered life. In return, it helped cure the sick and delivered oracles (predictions) for the priests. Of course, today, we figure that whatever the animals predicted was probably a lot of bull-oney.

During her reign, Cleopatra likely also participated in ceremonies for another important bull in Egyptian religion—the Apis, the incarnation of the creator god, Ptah. Archaeologists have found many mummified Apis and Buchis bulls in special burial chambers, including tombs for the mummified mothers of Apis bulls. We know that the Egyptian priests of Anubis mummified humans. But it makes us wonder—who mummified the bulls? Moo-ticians?

Within two years, king little bro and his gang took control of the throne and pushed queen big sis out—out of the palace, out of the city, out of her beloved Egypt.

But they had messed with the wrong sister. She may have been Queen of the Nile, but Cleopatra was no queen of denial. She knew what she had to do to regain her throne.

It's just that no one believed she had the guts to do it.

According to ancient Egyptian mythology, the first gods—Isis and Osiris—were brother-sister, husband-wife. Horus, their child, is in the middle.

© Jon Bodsworth

The Origin of Brother-Sister Marriages: Isis and Osiris

Sisters and brothers marrying? Ugh. We moderns gag at the very idea. But for ancient Egyptian royal families, it was as natural as the annual Nile flood—though its origins were just as murky.

It all started with the Egyptian main gods—Isis and Osiris. Osiris was a divine king who brought civilization to the lands of the Nile. His wife was his sister, Isis. Why were they married? Because there was no one else around who qualified! A god could only marry a goddess, you see. The pharaohs followed that custom forever after.

The weirdness (to our modern eyes, anyway) just kept growing from there. A jealous brother—Set or Seth—murdered Osiris. But sister-wife Isis recovered her brother-husband's body and magically got pregnant. She gave birth to Horus—the falcon-headed god.

Once grown, Horus avenged his father's murder. Horus kicked Set's sorry, throne-stealing backside into the desert, but not before losing an eye in the bloody battle. Thoth, the god of wisdom, recovered and returned the eye to Horus. Thoth sported the body of a man with the head of an ibis, a water bird of the Nile (no explanation for why the god of wisdom sported a birdbrain). But, thanks to Thoth and the return of his now magic eye, Horus restored his father. Osiris lived again, ruling as king of the underworld.

Whew! Got all that?

These complicated stories supported the Egyptians' belief in the concept of divine kingship. All pharaohs were the human embodiment of Horus, sharing in his divinity. When pharaohs died, they became fully divine, joining Osiris in the underworld.

Egyptian religion may have made brother-sister marriages seem "natural," but we know better. They served a political purpose: to keep the ruling family in control of the throne. It was a power play—one that, to us moderns anyway, seems powerfully gross!

"Yeah, You and Whose Army?"

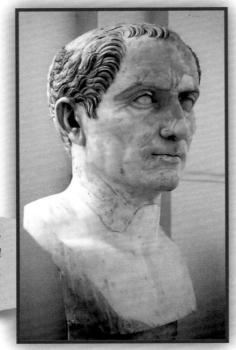

Cleopatra found a sneaky way to roll out the red carpet for her benefactor, Julius Caesar.

IMAGINE.

At an age when most of us get our first taste of true independence, Cleopatra found herself completely on her own, fleeing for her life and stuck alone on foreign soil.

But trying to keep Cleopatra away from her beloved Egypt was a bad idea. You'd have better luck keeping today's teen away from her cell phone.

In Syria, Cleopatra gathered an army to help her regain her throne. That's right—an *army*.

Remember, the queen was just out of her teens. Most of us at that age are just figuring out for the first time how to live without mommy and daddy. But Cleopatra whipped up a crowd of bloodthirsty warriors to fight on her behalf.

Whom did she recruit? And how did she convince them to fight for her? Nobody knows. But one thing is clear: This young queen knew how to take care of herself.

Cleopatra was about to turn getting kicked out into a reason for kicking butt.

Heads Will Roll!

Cleopatra stopped her march when she heard an amazing piece of news: her little brother had Pompey the Great—one of the most powerful leaders in Rome—beheaded on Egyptian soil. Talk about a bone-headed move.

Pompey got a big head winning many battles. He even named himself "the Great" (Magnus). He got cut down to size after Caesar won, though.

See, Rome was having a little power struggle of its own. Julius Caesar and Pompey the Great were fighting for control of Rome. For a while, it looked as if either man could win. Eventually, Caesar got the upper hand. He chased Pompey all the way to Greece and, finally, into Egypt.

Pompey sailed into the harbor of Alexandria, hoping to press Egypt into helping him fight off Caesar. After all, Pompey was a sort of a Roman

23

"Godfather" to the young king (Cleopatra's dad had appointed him guardian). He was virtually family, right?

Poor Pompey should've quit while he was ahead—or at least while he still had one. Because as soon as he stepped onto shore, the young king gave the order: slice off his head.

Why? The mini-king's advisers didn't want any part of Rome's war bleeding onto Egyptian soil. They figured eliminating one of the players would make the other one give up the chase. Good idea in theory. In practice? Not so much.

Their little head game backfired in a big way.

"You Did WHAT?"

The Egyptians thought they had done the right thing until Caesar basically said, "Heads! You lose." And all because Pompey (on coin) lost his.

Caesar arrived in Egypt looking for Pompey. But what he found there probably made him want to hurl. Especially when the boy king's advisers shoved Pompey's pickled head into his face. They likely expected a big, "You got him! Thanks!"

Instead, Caesar wept. That's right. Wept. He boo-hooed over the fall of one of Rome's great generals. Or at least that's what he said. He probably cried because *they* got the job done before he could.

Worse, Caesar didn't leave Egypt. Instead, he marched right into the palace and took over the biggest rooms for himself and his officers. To add insult to injury, he had his army of four thousand soldiers camp right outside the royal quarters.

The boy king and his advisers were furious. They'd done Caesar a favor. Why couldn't he just leave? Caesar claimed that since he was there, he might as well help "work things out" between the royal siblings. But the boy king's advisers claimed there was no problem—nope—no problem at all between the queen and the king.

So where was the young queen? The boy king and his advisers shrugged their shoulders, looking innocent. "Heck if we know."

But heck if Cleopatra was going to let them get away with a lie like that.

We're on a Roll Here

As soon as Cleopatra heard that Julius Caesar had parked at the palace, she realized that marching in an army might send the wrong message. What if Caesar thought she was attacking him?

No, she needed to talk to the great Caesar one-on-one. But how? Her brother had posted guards at every entrance into the city. This time, she knew they wouldn't hesitate to do to her what they had done to Pompey.

If she wanted to save her neck, she needed to do something unexpected. A surprise. Yes, a plan her brother could never imagine in a million years.

And the answer was right at her feet.

Cleopatra had herself jelly-rolled into a carpet and had one of her trusted servants smuggle her into the harbor on a rickety rowboat. Then—with the queen all snug in a rug—he marched her into the palace. "Present for Caesar," the servant claimed when questioned.

Once inside Caesar's room, the carpet was unrolled and out stepped the daring young queen.

We don't know how Caesar reacted, but we bet his first words went something close to this: "Um. *Wow!*"

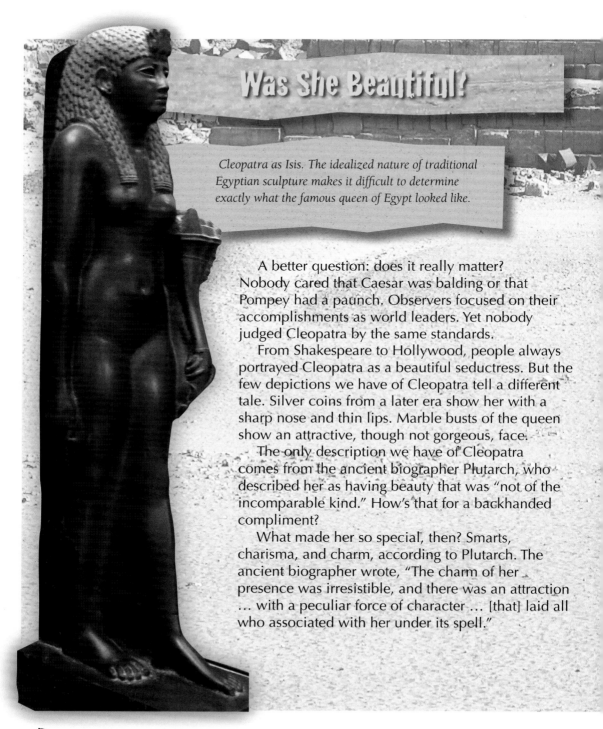

Was She Beautiful?

Cleopatra as Isis. The idealized nature of traditional Egyptian sculpture makes it difficult to determine exactly what the famous queen of Egypt looked like.

A better question: does it really matter? Nobody cared that Caesar was balding or that Pompey had a paunch. Observers focused on their accomplishments as world leaders. Yet nobody judged Cleopatra by the same standards.

From Shakespeare to Hollywood, people always portrayed Cleopatra as a beautiful seductress. But the few depictions we have of Cleopatra tell a different tale. Silver coins from a later era show her with a sharp nose and thin lips. Marble busts of the queen show an attractive, though not gorgeous, face.

The only description we have of Cleopatra comes from the ancient biographer Plutarch, who described her as having beauty that was "not of the incomparable kind." How's that for a backhanded compliment?

What made her so special, then? Smarts, charisma, and charm, according to Plutarch. The ancient biographer wrote, "The charm of her presence was irresistible, and there was an attraction … with a peculiar force of character … [that] laid all who associated with her under its spell."

Caesar was 52, married, and had a reputation for charming just about every woman he encountered, including the wives of enemies and friends. Yet Romans claimed the young queen somehow ensnared him. It is just as likely—if not more so, given Caesar's reputation—that Caesar worked his charm on the young queen rather than the other way around.

Turns out, our young queen was as compelling as a giant magnet in a room full of nails.

Still, the focus on what she looked like minimizes her visionary nature. Cleopatra tried to create a world where the East shared power with the West. She fought to keep her nation independent in a world that was rapidly becoming all Roman. And she yearned to strengthen and preserve her country's ancient heritage. Had she succeeded, the world would probably look very different today.

Given all that, does it even matter what she looked like?

Caesar was fifty-two years old. He had a wife at home and a grown daughter who had died giving birth years before. He was balding. Yet the dude had a reputation for being a player. Go figure.

It wasn't long before the two were an item.

When king little bro found out they had teamed up in more ways than one, he threw a royal tantrum. Literally. He ran outside the gates of the palace, hurled his crown, and screamed that he had been double-crossed.

Real mature, right? You'd think the Egyptians would've been embarrassed for their king. Instead, they surrounded him and egged him on. It was the Romans' fault! Down with the Romans!

Caesar's soldiers dragged the purple-faced, screaming preteen back into the palace. But the damage was done. Angry mobs surrounded the palace, cursing Caesar and the Romans.

Things may have been heating up between Caesar and Cleopatra, but they were getting downright blistering in the streets of Alexandria.

Fight! Fight!

The little king and his advisers whipped up an anti-Rome frenzy. They spread rumors that Cleopatra was going to hand Egypt over to the Romans (as if). Now the people of Alexandria hated Caesar *and* Cleopatra.

A mob gathered to storm the palace. Caesar calmed everybody by promising he'd give Cyprus back to Egypt. In those days, small countries were traded like baseball cards. And like baseball cards, some were more valuable than others. Cyprus, on the whole, was not necessarily top-drawer pick. But it wasn't a bench warmer, either.

You have to remember that Rome wanted to be "Masters of the World." Their game was getting more territory, not giving any away. So why would Caesar offer it? Some scholars think the young queen put the idea in Caesar's head. After all, it was her father who lost Cyprus when he did nothing to stop a Roman invasion of that formerly Egyptian-held territory. Getting it back proved the young queen's mettle and strength. Cleopatra worked toward a single goal: to keep Egypt as powerful and independent as possible. And that meant getting back the lands Egypt once ruled.

She was consistent, too. Cleopatra never let a negotiation opportunity slip by without grabbing more territory for her kingdom—from this point on until her death. Cyprus was just the beginning.

Still, it didn't matter who came up with the idea. To the Egyptians, it was too little too late. They saw Cleopatra's partnership with Caesar as betrayal. So her little sister, Arsinoe, stepped up and proclaimed herself the true queen of Egypt.

A claim that meant war.

Cleopatra's response? Bring it on, little sister. Bring it on.

Did savvy negotiator Cleopatra convince Caesar to return Cyprus to Egypt?

Transporting grain on the Nile. Egypt was often called the "Breadbasket of Rome" because it provided most of the region's grain.

During Cleopatra's era, kingdoms around Egypt fell to Rome faster than a teenage boy reaching for his game controller. Greece, Syria, Lebanon, Judea—all ended up under Roman rule. Farther west, Spain and parts of what are now France and Germany also caved to the Romans. Egypt was definitely feeling the squeeze.

Yet Egypt remained independent in the face of Roman domination. Why? Partly because Rome depended on Egypt's grain exports. Nobody wanted to risk losing their daily bread if the Egyptians resisted.

But the real reason Rome didn't put the hurt on Egypt? Turns out the Romans were scared. Not of Egypt's puff-pastry army, but of what could happen if the wrong guy took over the territory. Egypt was so rich that Romans feared it could corrupt the wrong Roman. What if someone used Egypt's riches to bankroll yet another civil war?

Egypt never took up arms against Rome. Smart move. After all, fighting Rome was like taunting a grizzly bear. The best you could do was irritate the beast. The worst? Get a one-way ticket out of its digestive track.

Cleopatra's little brother—and soon her little sister—forgot that little piece of wisdom. They really thought they could push out Rome. Cleopatra had a better idea: partner up and share.

For a little while, it looked as if her plan just might work.

Family Feud

Cleopatra's father, Ploemy XII, likely hoped his kids wouldn't fight for power. Silly man.

CLEOPATRA'S LITTLE SISTER, ARSINOE,
and little brother Ptolemy XIII wanted a piece of the power pie for themselves. That meant getting rid of Cleopatra. So the pair trashed-talked her worse than feuding starlets at a Hollywood club. The locals—tired of paying huge taxes to

31

pay off the Romans (remember the Piper's deals?)—liked having someone to blame for all of their problems. They jumped at the chance to point the finger at Cleopatra and attack the Romans.

But really. Taking Rome on in war? What were they thinking? Yeah, Caesar had only four thousand men, and they had a whole city full of ticked-off citizens, but still. We're talking the Romans here—four thousand of the most highly disciplined, well-trained killers the ancient world had ever seen, led by possibly the most brilliant general since Alexander the Great.

It was like watching an elf take on the NBA's biggest star in a dunking contest.

Ships That Burn in the Night

Arsinoe and Ptolemy's misguided advisers pushed the Egyptians to attack Caesar by land and sea in Alexandria. Caesar and his men, along with Cleopatra, hunkered down to defend the palace. The odds didn't look good. Caesar and Cleopatra were vastly outnumbered.

But Caesar wasn't known as an awesome general for nothing. He and his

© Ziad Nour

men took action. They cut through the mob of Egyptian soldiers like hungry teens on the way to the food court.

It didn't take long for Caesar to seize the lighthouse at Alexandria—one of the Seven Wonders of the Ancient World—giving him control of the harbor. Only one problem: he accidentally torched a warehouse of precious scrolls headed for the Great Library of Alexandria. Oops!

Imagine him trying to explain that "little mistake" to Cleopatra.

Sink or Swim

After burning down the library warehouse, Caesar found himself trapped in the harbor. He escaped by jumping onto one of his boats anchored there. But so many of his men followed him, the boat began to sink. So Caesar jumped into the choppy water and swam to a boat farther out to sea. Not bad for an old geezer.

Ancient Alexandria, re-imagined. Today, almost all of the splendor of the ancient harbor lies at the bottom of the sea.

Books on a Stick

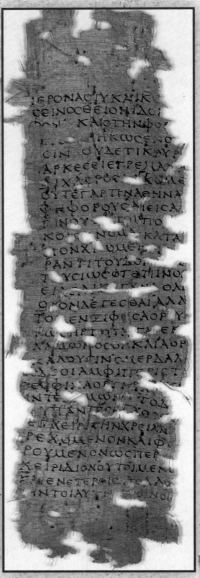

Most ancient books were actually rolled-up scrolls. This Egyptian scroll bears the Greek writing common to the Ptolemaic period. Funny fact: many scholars believe the ancients did not read silently, but recited aloud, even if they were only reading to themselves.

Cleopatra's city totally rocked. When it came to books, it rolled too. See, all of the books at the Library of Alexandria were actually scrolls—rolled-up papyrus or parchment sheets.

The famous library started when the first Ptolemy pharaoh got a little greedy—for books. He wanted to own every book ever written. He sent a letter to all the world leaders asking them for copies of all their stories, poems, and histories. Then he had every ship sailing into Alexandria searched for scrolls. Librarian thugs snatched the scrolls off the ships, recopied them, and then returned them—but not the originals. They kept those for the library!

Over the generations, the library grew to house more than 700,000 scrolls. It would take two thousand years before a library came anywhere near to having as many titles. Today, the biggest library in the world is the Library of Congress in Washington, D.C., which houses more than 32 million books.

The Library at Alexandria also housed a science center and museum, which attracted—over the centuries—some of the greatest thinkers in the ancient world, including Euclid, the inventor of geometry; Aristothenes, the great mathematician; Hagnodice, the first Greek

female doctor (the first Egyptian one, Peseshet, had come on the scene two thousand years earlier); Eratosthenes, the geographer; Archimedes, the brilliant inventor; and many others.

Julius Caesar may have set the library warehouse on fire during his war against Cleopatra's brother, but the library itself continued thriving. Several fires over the centuries eventually took it down, though. All those priceless books up in smoke— what a burning shame!

The New Library of Alexandria was rebuilt near what was thought to be the original site of the ancient library. And like the original, it houses multiple research centers, scientific museums, and a vast collection of books.

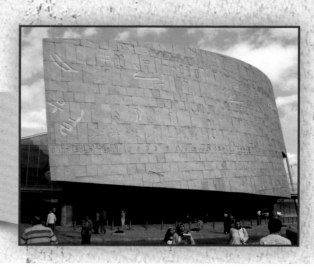

It Was All Greek to Her

Cleopatra read most books in Greek, the main language of government and business in Egypt during the reign of her family, the Ptolemies.

But could she read hieroglyphics, too? Given Cleopatra's talent for languages and ability to speak Egyptian, our best guess is . . .

Hieroglyphics, Egypt's ancient form of writing, was in use 3,000 years before Cleopatra ruled. Over the centuries, even as other forms of writing developed in Egypt, hieroglyphics remained important for religious, funerary, and official texts.

After the Romans took over Egypt, knowledge of the stylized picture-writing began to fade. Why did the Romans find it so difficult to read hieroglyphics? Maybe they just couldn't "picture" it.

In modern times, we learned to decode hieroglyphics thanks to one of Cleopatra's ancestors. Ptolemy V wrote a decree on a piece of granite we call the Rosetta Stone, written in three languages—Greek, Demotic (a kind of Egyptian cursive), and hieroglyphics.

Scholars knew how to read the ancient Greek but nobody could figure out the other two. Eventually, someone broke the code for Demotic. When they realized the message was identical to the one in Greek, they knew the hieroglyphics would be too. And the rest, as they say, is history.

Can you read hieroglyphics like Cleopatra? Use the template below to read the hieroglyphic answer to the following joke:

What is a mummy's favorite type of music?

X A O S M R E C P Y

Still, Caesar faced an onslaught of furious Egyptians. Arrows and spears flew, nearly blotting out the bright Egyptian sun. Just when it looked as if Caesar might actually lose the war, Caesar's reinforcements from Syria arrived, saving the day. Like any good mob boss, Caesar always had a group of lackeys ready to strong-arm his enemies.

Little brother king tried to escape by swimming across the Nile but drowned. And little sister traitor Arsinoe was arrested. As the dust cleared, only one ruler of Egypt was left standing: Cleopatra. And—we can imagine—she stood triumphant with one hand on her hip and the other with fingers snapping high in the air.

The message? *I'm* the star of this show, baby!

The Grand Tour

Talk about the royal tour! Cleopatra took Caesar on a cruise of the Nile, showing off her nation's treasures.

After the smackdown of her younger brother and sister, Cleopatra took Caesar on a tour of Egypt. Not just any tour, but a beautiful cruise down the Nile on her royal barge. Egyptians swarmed to the banks to wish them well. They had better. Followed by four hundred Roman soldiers, her barge was the lead in the "Don't Mess with Us" parade of power.

But it was also Cleopatra's moment to shine—she showed off her country's legacy to the world's strongest leader. Rome at the time was largely a city of mud and brick. We can only imagine Caesar's awe as he looked upon the pyramids and giant temples for the first time. And we can only imagine how impressed he would have been at the way the Egyptians treated their queen. Because she had emerged triumphant, the people bowed down to her as if she were the goddess they believed her to be. They called her the new Isis. Soon they began calling Caesar her Osiris.

Her Nile cruise was a great gift to Caesar. But what Cleopatra gave him next left the whole world speechless.

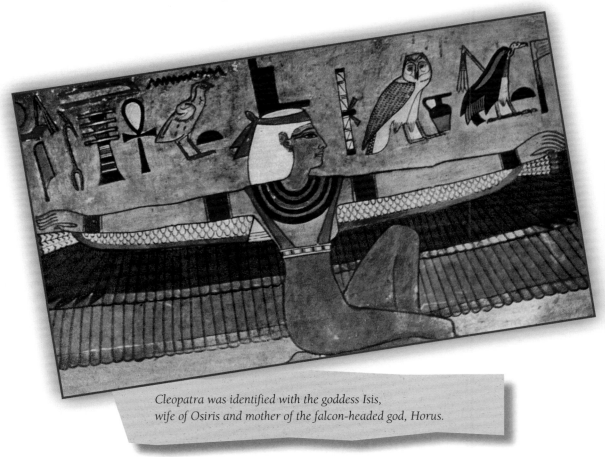

Cleopatra was identified with the goddess Isis, wife of Osiris and mother of the falcon-headed god, Horus.

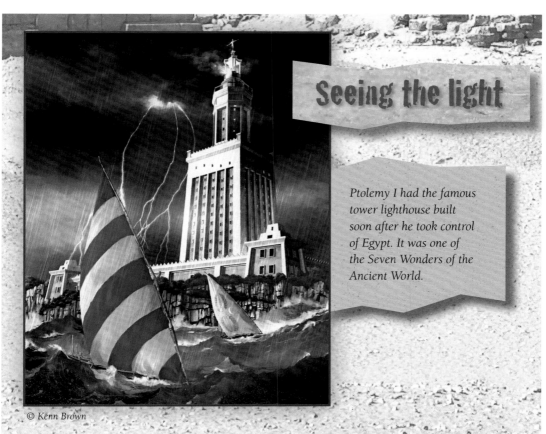

Seeing the light

© Kenn Brown

Ptolemy I had the famous tower lighthouse built soon after he took control of Egypt. It was one of the Seven Wonders of the Ancient World.

The Lighthouse of Alexandria stood about forty-five stories high and looked like a mini-skyscraper (imagine a fatter, shorter Empire State building). At the top of the lighthouse stood an immense twelve-foot mirror of polished metal, reflecting the sun during the day and fires at night. The reflected light, some said, could be seen miles away.

The lighthouse became a huge tourist attraction. The lower level served as a "food court." Vendors probably sold souvenirs, too. After all, even in ancient times, no vacation was complete without fast food and cheap trinkets!

The lighthouse stood for 1,500 years. An earthquake in 1326 toppled it into the sea. Today, deep-sea-diving archaeologists are trying to recover the ancient stones. Luckily for us, their "fire" for discovering the great lighthouse never went out.

The Julian Calendar? Please. It Was Cleo's

Cleopatra's court astronomers helped Caesar fix the messed-up Roman calendar. The Egyptians had used a more accurate solar calendar for eons. But Caesar took all the credit when he brought it to Rome.

Everybody credits Caesar for fixing the Roman calendar and starting huge building projects. But how come nobody noticed that he started these projects only after spending time in Egypt with Cleopatra and her court of top mathematicians and scientists?

Until Caesar adopted the Egyptian solar calendar, the Roman calendar was a mess. Roman priests in charge of the lunar-based calendar inserted days—and sometimes whole months—to keep it on track. Occasionally, they changed the calendar to keep a favored politician in power, sometimes even changing election dates or bribing officers to look the other way. As a result, the Roman calendar was always "off." Imagine a fall harvest festival ending up in December or the summer solstice taking place in early spring and you get the idea.

Meanwhile, the Egyptians had long ago created a solar calendar. Caesar learned about her more reliable calendar from Cleopatra's astronomer and took it back to Rome, replacing the empire's calendar.

In the Middle Ages, the Julian calendar was tweaked a bit more and renamed the Gregorian calendar—the calendar we use today. And we can all thank the Egyptians for the breakthrough!

4

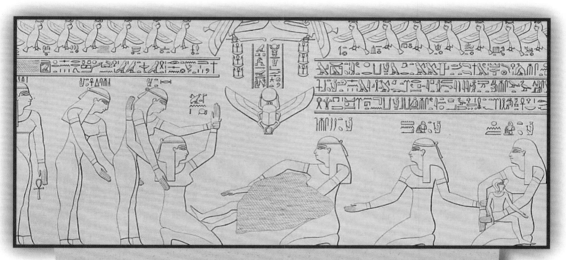

Some new moms give their baby a rattle. Cleopatra gave hers a temple. She built the Temple at Armant (above, showing Isis giving birth to Horus) in honor of her firstborn.

SURPRISE! CLEOPATRA GAVE CAESAR

a special present: a baby boy. She named the baby Caesarion (see-*zare*-ee-un), which meant "Little Caesar." Suddenly, "we deliver" had an entirely different meaning.

41

The Queen of Egypt and the Ruler of Rome having a baby? The people of Egypt thought it was a great thing. After all, Caesar was less likely to attack now that he was "family," right?

The Romans? Not so thrilled.

Remember, Caesar already had a wife—Calpurnia—in Rome. His one daughter from a previous marriage—Julia—had died years before. A son could tie Caesar to the Egyptian queen in a way nothing else could—which is exactly what the Romans feared.

So when Caesar brought Cleopatra and their love baby home to meet the Romans, it didn't go so great. For the most part, they greeted her with as much warmth as a cat tripping over a nest of snakes. Only there was more hissing.

Calpurnia, Caesar's wife, could not have been too happy about Cleopatra coming into town, baby in tow.

A Roman Holiday to Die For

Caesar brought Cleopatra to Rome and set her up, with their new baby, in his gorgeous villa across the Tiber River. When he wasn't with Cleopatra, he hung out at home with his Roman wife as if nothing had changed. The Romans couldn't have been more outraged!

Then, adding insult to injury, he placed a golden statue of Cleopatra in a new temple of Venus he had specially built.

Putting his foreign girlfriend on a pedestal was one thing, but what Caesar

Caesar had Cleopatra stay in his villa outside the city because…well, his wife might not have appreciated the other option. Also, it was Roman law that no monarch could stay within Rome's city walls.

did next really got the Romans twisting in their togas. He tried to pass a law that allowed Roman men to marry foreign women for the purpose of producing children. What was he saying? That he wanted his half-Egyptian son recognized as a legitimate heir—and potential future ruler of Rome? That was the last straw.

Caesar had taken a do-or-die gamble. And his senator "friends" chose "die." Twenty-six senators knifed Caesar to death at a senate meeting. What a way to get your point across!

Caesar probably wished his senate "friends" hadn't been such "sticklers" for making their point.

43

Animal pull toys—in the shape of cats, frogs, or crocodiles—were popular in ancient Egypt.

© Maru Harrsch

© Kathleen Cohen

Caesarion and other ancient Egyptian kids played with toys that looked a lot like the kind you played with when you were little. As babies, they played with rattles, clappers, and pull toys. As they grew, they played with dolls with movable limbs, changeable clothes, and long fake hair (think Barbie—except without all that plastic).

Older kids played with spinning tops and clay animals as well as with balls of all sizes. Girls seemed to prefer juggling, while boys played rough games, such as wrestling and jumping games, where the object was to "take down" the jumper.

Egyptian kids and adults also played board games. The most popular was a game called Senet. Nobody has been able to figure out how to play it exactly, but most think it was like a complicated form of Chutes and Ladders. Many kids also had pets, including cats, dogs, and monkeys. Every kid knew that cats deserved special care. They were sacred to the Egyptians. If a house cat died, for example, everyone in the family shaved their eyebrows in mourning. And if you killed a cat on purpose, you faced the death penalty. *Meow-ch!*

Senet may just be the oldest board game in the world, dating back to 3,500 BCE. The famous King Tutankhamen of the 18th dynasty—a thousand years before Cleopatra's time—had four Senet games buried with him in his tomb.

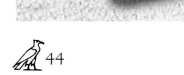

For Cleopatra, stuck in Rome, Caesar's death must have seemed like a nightmare. Could she get out of Rome with her young son quickly enough to escape Caesar's fate?

Caesar's death left Cleopatra with a great big mess. Suddenly, being the mother of the only son of Rome's *murdered* ruler didn't seem like such a prize. Plus, Caesar had not succeeded in passing the law that would have recognized her as his foreign wife and Caesarion as his legitimate heir. Stuck in his villa with Caesar's enemies whooping it up on the streets, Cleopatra probably felt like a bull's-eye target in a room full of twitchy archers.

So she did the only thing that made sense: she packed up and left. But she didn't go home to cry on the couch. Like any good ruler, she wanted to make sure her new territories weren't rocked by events in Rome. So on her way home she stopped by Cyprus.

Remember how Caesar had given Cyprus back to her earlier? She wanted the people of Cyprus to stay loyal to her and Egypt. Even under duress, the young queen kept her eye on the prize—making Egypt bigger and stronger. Fortunately, the people of Cyprus loved her. They embraced her warmly and issued coins bearing her image.

Rome, meanwhile, teetered on self-destruction. Who would take charge? Would the Senate reassert the power of the republic? Or would yet another power-hungry general take over as a tyrant?

But when Caesar's will was finally read aloud, *everybody* gasped.

45

Why the Romans Hated Cleopatra

Cicero hated Cleopatra for many reasons, not the least of which was that he thought it "abnormal" for a woman to rule. Also, she forgot to send him a book he wanted.

Imagine it from the Romans' point of view. Caesar was married. The guy was old. He was shaking things up as the sole ruler of their country, possibly destroying the republic. And then he had the gall to march home with a young queen and their love baby in tow?

It was just too much for the conservative Romans.

Remember, too, that Roman culture celebrated the quiet woman who hid away in the home. Romans didn't know what to make of a bold young queen more educated than most of their senators, sharper than most of their scholars, and more confident and glamorous than anyone they'd ever met.

Cleopatra's very presence shook their world.

Still, most Romans were intensely curious about the young queen. They clamored for invitations to Caesar's villa to check out the brilliant young monarch. Most were dazzled. But one powerful senator named Cicero wrote that he hated her. Why?

Cleopatra promised him a special scroll, but in the chaos after Caesar's murder, she forgot to send it to him. Talk about getting all wound up over nothing!

Untried and untested, the teenaged Octavian seemed like a strange choice to succeed the great Julius Caesar. At least, that's what Mark Antony thought.

Caesar had appointed his nephew, eighteen-year-old Octavian, as heir. Romans panicked. What had Caesar been thinking? The kid was … well, a kid! Totally unproven. He'd never led an army, let alone held political office. Was this some kind of joke?

Nobody was angrier at Caesar's choice than his top general and right-hand man, Mark Antony.

Antony was a seasoned warrior and politician. Caesar should've appointed him, he claimed, not some snot-nosed, knobby-kneed, pimply-faced peon who could barely hold a sword. Most senators agreed.

But Caesar's will was clear. He had adopted Octavian as his own son and heir. The Romans had no choice but to accept him.

47

Still, it didn't go down easily. To avoid yet another civil war, Octavian, Antony, and a general named Lepidus shared power equally. They formed a triumvirate—a three-person leadership.

Meanwhile, Antony wanted to conquer Parthia (the ancient Iran-Iraq region) and come back a war hero, kicking the snot-nosed kid—Octavian—out of power in Rome. But Octavian always found a way to undermine Antony.

Antony needed money, men, and supplies to conquer the Middle East. But Octavian never sent them. It was almost as if he wanted Antony to fail. Antony, however, refused to give up. If Octavian wouldn't help him, he would find somebody who would.

So he turned his sights on the wealthiest ally he knew—the queen of Egypt.

He figured he could easily manipulate Cleopatra to his will. After all, he represented the might of Rome. Cleopatra would bow down before him, just as most everybody else had, right?

Right?

Octavian, depicted as pharaoh in this temple wall, was a tougher opponent than either Antony or Cleopatra imagined.

A Spectacular Entrance

As one of the most powerful men in Rome, Antony thought he could easily manipulate and control the Queen of Egypt. He would soon learn otherwise.

ANTONY MAY HAVE BEEN A HEAVY HITTER

in the ancient world, but when it came to creating an entrance, he was a total lightweight—at least compared with Cleopatra.

Here's what happened: Antony sent a message to the queen, commanding her to meet him in Tarsus, a city in what is now Turkey, near Syria. People whispered that she had supported one of the men who had killed Caesar (as if). He wanted her to answer for herself. Was he hoping the accusation of betrayal would scare her into acting all subservient? Who knows?

You can pretty much bet he wasn't expecting what he *did* get: a royal diss.

Cleopatra ignored his letters and took her own sweet time obeying his summons. Her message to Antony was clear: you may be one of the most powerful men in Rome, but "you're not the boss of me!"

Just for good measure, she put on an "in your face" display of wealth and power that had everybody gaping in wonder.

The Arrival of the Queen

Cleopatra's boat floated up the river in Tarsus like an image from a dream. Gold gleamed off the cabins, and purple sails billowed in the wind. Rowers paddled silver oars in time to the hypnotic sounds of pipes, flutes, and lutes.

Cleopatra, dressed as Venus, lay beneath a canopy of gold cloth, while boys costumed as Cupid stood on either side, fanning her. Beautiful girls posed as minor goddesses and sea nymphs burned sweet incense to perfume the air around them.

Decked out as a goddess, Cleopatra made everybody weak in the knees. But it wasn't just for show. To the Egyptians, she *was* Isis, the main goddess of Egypt. And, as in a religious experience, everyone was hushed in awe at the sight of the goddess-queen.

Nobody—and we mean nobody—could quite pull off an entrance like Cleopatra.

Antony, who had been judging cases in the city center when Cleopatra arrived, heard the commotion at the dock. He looked up and found himself alone. Everybody, it seemed, had run to the river to catch a glimpse of the magnetic queen.

But Antony was the boss man. He wasn't going to run to the queen like everybody else. She had to come to him. He had a message sent to Cleopatra: join him for dinner in his quarters. Tonight. The answer came back: *No. You come here and dine with me.*

The smart queen wanted home-field—or at least home-boat—advantage. Being a friendly kind of guy, Antony obeyed … er, agreed. He went to her. When he stood in front of her boat, he couldn't believe his eyes. So many twinkling, shimmering lights decorated the boat, it looked as though Cleopatra had captured the heavens just for him.

Antony was up the plank faster than a pirate lunging for treasure.

Antony didn't want to rock the boat by refusing Cleopatra's offer for dinner on her barge.

Obsession by Any Other Name

William Shakespeare, also captivated by Plutarch's description of Cleopatra's spectacular entrance, wrote it into his play, Antony and Cleopatra.

Plutarch's description of Cleopatra's visit to Mark Antony fired everyone's imagination—from Shakespeare to Hollywood. Here's how Will described her entrance in *Antony and Cleopatra:*

> The barge she sat in, like a burnish'd throne,
> Burnt on the water. The poop was beaten gold,
> Purple of the sails, and so perfumed that
> The winds were love-sick with them; the oars were silver,
> Which to the tune of flutes kept stroke, and made
> The water which they beat to follow faster,
> As amorous of their strokes. For her own person,
> It beggar'd all description: she did lie
> In her pavilion—cloth of gold, of tissue—
> O'er-picturing that Venus where we see
> The fancy outwork nature.
>
> (act 2, scene 2, lines 191–201)

Any woman who could make even the winds "love-sick" rocked. But overall, Cleopatra did not fare so well in the English bard's play. Some modern commentators say Shakespeare made her seem "histrionic" (which means "over-the-top silly") and "even faintly ridiculous" in many scenes. The last great queen of Egypt, in Shakespeare's hands, often comes across as a spoiled, pouting, selfish creature rather than a strong leader determined to do what was best for her country.

Shakespeare also calls the great queen "a piece of work" (act 1, scene 1). Today, we use that phrase to describe someone who is outrageous—and usually in a bad way.

Cleopatra came off even worse in another famous play, *Caesar and Cleopatra*, by George Bernard Shaw. Shaw portrayed the young Cleopatra—upon first meeting Caesar—as a silly, frightened young girl. He even had Caesar call her kitten. Yet this so-called kitten had been ruling her country—virtually by herself— for three years when she met the powerful Roman. She had raised an army in a foreign land to fight for her crown. And she had outwitted her brother's forces, avoiding assassination, to meet with Caesar.

The real Cleopatra was likely more of a roaring lioness than a helpless kitten. But you wouldn't have gotten that from the playwrights who rewrote her history— even if you read between the "lions!"

VIVIEN LEIGH

THE "SCARLETT O'HARA" OF THE NILE

in

CAESAR and CLEOPATRA

A TEMPTATION in

TECHNICOLOR

Dining in Style

Cleopatra knew how to throw a party, too. An endless supply of sumptuous food and tasty wine flowed to Antony and his men—and kept flowing—all the way back to her palace in Alexandria.

The queen's power parties were legendary. One story had the queen make a bet with Antony that she could outspend him on a party. Antony laughed. Clearly, she had never seen one of his banquets. It was on!

Cleopatra threw a typical party. Antony smirked. That was it? That was all the game she had?

Cleopatra's response: just wait. She signaled her servant, who placed a cup of wine vinegar before her. She pulled off one of her enormous pearl earrings and dropped it—with a flourish—into the cup. Antony gaped in horror.

See, the Romans thought pearls were the rarest, most beautiful gems ever. Her giant pearl was virtually priceless in the eyes of a Roman.

 54

Cleopatra gave the concoction a little swirl—showing Antony how the pearl had dissolved. Then she downed it. Antony's eyes must have bugged out in astonishment. It was clear the queen's "taste" for expensive jewelry had a whole new meaning. When she reached for the other earring, one of Antony's friends stayed her hand.

Cleopatra had won. He could not match her wealth—or nerve.

It's a great story, but it likely didn't happen that way (if it happened at all), especially since it takes about twenty four hours for a pearl to dissolve in vinegar. Still, the legend tells us a lot about Roman perception of the Egyptian queen. For some, the story became a symbol for the destructive and seductive power of Egypt's riches. For others, it showed a queen unwilling to bend to the might of Rome. It's as if she'd actually said, "What you think is awesome is nothing to me—I can devour it in a single gulp."

It's the kind of legend that perfectly captured Rome's fear of Egypt's "mystery." But for Antony, it wasn't a mystery at all.

It was another excuse to party.

Pearl or no pearl, Cleopatra's legendary parties impressed the party-loving Antony.

Egyptian Jewelry— Bling on a String

Protection as good as gold—the Egyptians believed jewelry had magical powers to keep you safe.

© Jon Bodsworth

For us, jewelry is mostly about looking pretty or showing status. For the ancient Egyptians, it was all that *and* a form of fancy magic. You know how in old legends garlic kept vampires away? Well, jewelry often was to the Egyptians what garlic was to people afraid of vampires. It kept evil away and protected them from bad luck, which is why most Egyptians rocked more bling than headliners at a rap concert.

Necklaces, collars, bracelets, earrings, anklets, headdresses, belts, rings—the Egyptians wore it all. They figured the more jewelry you put on, the safer you were from bad things happening. That's why so many pharaohs buried themselves with enough gold to sink a barge on the Nile. Their gold, they hoped, would give them glory in the afterlife. But, for the most part, it only served to "glorify" tomb robbers' pockets!

Almost every piece of jewelry had some sort of symbolic meaning or magical power. Amulets came in the shape of animals, gods, or symbols for protection. Gold connected you to Ra, the sun god, for example; while lapis lazuli, turquoise, and other blue-green colors connected you to the life-giving, renewing powers of the Nile.

And if Egyptians couldn't afford the good stuff, they opted for fabulous fakes. Egyptian jewelers made glass beads look like precious stones (the Romans did this also). The Egyptian hieroglyph for *bead* meant "luck." Lucky for them, there were many beads and jewels from which to choose!

A Roman Redneck

If Antony were alive today, he'd be the kind of "good ol' boy" whose idea of fun was seeing how many soda cans he could crush against his head before passing out. He was a "guy's guy" who loved to fight, drink, and laugh. The sophisticated, elegant Cleopatra played along with him, joining him in his games, drinking, and parties.

At the palace, they started a group called Those That Live the Inimitable Life, devoted to living life to the fullest. Their idea of a good time? Dressing like poor people and going into bad parts of the city. Sometimes, Antony picked fights with people at dive bars just so he could see their reactions when he identified himself and the queen. For some reason, the pair found this hilarious.

Their bodyguards? Not amused. But Cleopatra's cleverness had even Antony's own soldiers laughing into their helmets.

No matter how silly Antony could seem, Cleopatra always found a way to make him look good. She was said to have had "a thousand" ways to charm and flatter. Take the day Antony and Cleopatra went fishing. Poor Antony couldn't catch a single fish. Well, he couldn't let the Queen of the Nile see that!

So he secretly paid off a fisherman to dive into the water and hook his recently caught fish on Antony's line. When Antony brought up his "catch," everybody acted all impressed, including Cleopatra. She did not let on, however, that she had caught on to his lame trick.

The next day Cleopatra convinced him to go fishing again, this time with a boatload of friends. When Antony threw his line, she secretly ordered one of her own servants to dive in and place a *dried* fish on his hook. When Antony pulled up his salted prize, everybody burst out laughing.

Once again, Cleopatra had one-upped her Roman partner. But instead of rubbing it in, she turned the situation into a compliment.

"Emperor," she said, "you had better give up your fishing to us poor rulers. Your sport is to hunt cities and kingdoms and continents."

She knew how to keep a man hooked, that's for sure.

Roman Outrage

Meanwhile, Romans raged over Antony's antics. Wasn't he supposed to be fighting Rome's enemies in Parthia? While Antony and Cleopatra canoodled and played tricks, the Parthians invaded Roman-controlled Syria. Why wasn't Antony doing anything about it?

To the rest of the world, it looked as if Rome's greatest general had turned into a love-sick puppy. Or, at least, that's the message Octavian pumped out of his propaganda machine: Cleopatra had "bewitched" Antony. She had him wrapped around her little finger.

Cleopatra as pharaoh (right), making offering to Isis and Horus.

But it wasn't true. Despite all their fun and games, the pair did indeed hash out an arrangement for the future. It went beyond Antony's plans to conquer Parthia. They created a plan in which a strengthened Egypt partnered with Rome (instead of becoming its slave). They aimed to create a more stable, unified relationship between the West and the East.

Too bad for them, Octavian had an entirely different plan.

Cleopatra Wrote the Book on Egyptian Cosmetics

Okay, maybe not *the* book, but a book. According to legend, Cleopatra wrote a book on the proper use of Egyptian cosmetics. The queen of Egypt was supposedly an expert at using makeup to enhance her looks. In fact, one ancient Roman called her a "fatal beauty daubed with unguents" (meaning she enhanced her already good looks with makeup).

Both men and women wore makeup in ancient Egypt. Makeup even had spiritual meaning. According to one selection from the *Book of the Dead* (a series of prayers and guidelines for making it safely into the underworld), a man must meet his fate—the judgment of death—"painted with eye paint [and] anointed with the finest oil of myrrh."

No telling what might happen if his makeup was smudged!

Kohl, the dark, eyeliner-like makeup worn around the eyes by both men and women, was made by grinding green malachite and mixing it with lead compounds. Yes, lead. They didn't know it was brain poison. Then they mixed the powder with duck or chicken fat for easy spreading. Greasy goodness!

To give blush to their cheeks, lips, and nails, they ground red ochre and mixed it with water. Egyptians were famous throughout the ancient world for their sweet-smelling perfumes. They even honored a healer god of perfume—Nefertem.

Egyptians used cosmetic spoons to mix lead powder with duck fat to make black eyeliner, or khol. This spoon from the New Kingdom features a woman swimming by holding onto a duck. What should we call her— a duck driver?

You Won't Be-weave This!

The busts of Cleopatra created during her lifetime show her wearing her hair in the Greek fashion: long hair wound up in a bun at the back. However, archaeologists have found that even thousands of years before Cleopatra, Egyptians wore hair extensions and wigs. Men, too. Seems as if Egypt anticipated Hollywood weaves by four-thousand-plus years.

How do we know the Egyptians rocked hair extensions? Archaeologists have found mummies with false hair woven into real locks. Plus researchers have discovered amazing double-style wigs featuring both tight plaits and colored curls. They've also found mummies sporting red hair dye (henna) covering graying locks. Between wigs, hair extensions, and hair dye, the Egyptians never had an excuse for a bad hair day.

No small hairpieces for the Egyptians—they liked wigs so much they sometimes doubled the fun! The double wig, right, comes from the 11th Dynasty, while the jeweled wig is from the 19th Dynasty, both thousands of years before Cleopatra.

© Jon Bodsworth

The Sun and the Moon

Octavia, Antony's fourth wife, likely hoped to keep the peace between her power-hungry little brother, Octavian, and hot-headed husband, Antony.

OCTAVIAN ACTED AS IF CLEOPATRA WAS kryptonite to Antony's Superman. He even claimed that Cleopatra had weakened Antony for war—that she had sapped his will to fight. Nothing could be further from the truth. Once the pair negotiated what Antony needed from her to win his war—and what Egypt would get in return—Antony left for the battlefield.

Six months later, Cleopatra gave birth to twins—Alexander Helios (the Sun) and Cleopatra Selene (the Moon). Now the Queen of Egypt was the mother of three children, counting Caesarion, her son with Caesar.

Antony would not see Cleopatra again or meet their children for another three and a half years. What took him so long to get back to her?

First, he threw himself into preparing for his invasion of Parthia. But just as he was about to launch the campaign, he received an urgent message to return to Rome. A war had broken out between his supporters and Octavian's forces.

You won't believe who started it!

This Time, It Really Was a Women's Fault

Antony's third wife, Fulvia, started a war on his behalf! Antony, it seems, liked the take-charge kind of woman.

Fulvia, Antony's Roman wife, started the war in Rome. Yes, you read that right. Like Caesar before him, Antony was married! His Roman wife, Fulvia, attempted a takeover on Antony's behalf.

The strong-willed Fulvia likely hoped that by taking out Octavian, her hubby wouldn't need Cleopatra or her resources. But it didn't work. Octavian crushed her little rebellion. Soon after the coup attempt, Fulvia became sick and died.

Antony hurried back to Rome to clean up the mess. He convinced Octavian that he had no part in the uprising, and the two leaders made up. They reconfirmed their triumvirate. Only this time they divided the Roman pie three ways: Octavian took Rome and the West, Antony grabbed the East, and Lepidus held Africa. But Lepidus wasn't a real player—Octavian snatched Africa back before Lepidus could say "I hunt hyenas" five times fast. The real contest was between Antony and Octavian. This time, Octavian had a new trick up his sleeve.

"Marry My Sister or Else!"

To keep the peace, Octavian "gave" Antony his sister, Octavia, in marriage. It was an offer Antony couldn't refuse. If he'd said no, it likely would have resulted in immediate warfare between the two leaders. Antony wasn't ready for that.

So he married again.

Cleopatra's response? We have no record.

All we know is that she stayed busy running her country. Besides keeping her nation stable, she faced the added challenge of a more aggressive Parthia breathing down her territorial neck.

Antony, for his part, grew increasingly miserable. Octavian had scammed him. With the arranged political marriage came an agreement between the men to help each other. Antony promised ships for Octavian's navy, while Octavian promised 20,000 soldiers for Antony's campaign in Parthia. Over time, Antony delivered his ships. Octavian delivered nothing.

After several years with Octavia, Antony got antsy. He still hadn't toppled Octavian, and he still hadn't drummed up the resources he needed to fight in Parthia.

So, he decided the time was right to renew his alliance with Cleopatra. He needed her money—and her backing.

But there was just one little problem. He was still married to his enemy's sister. What in the world was he going to do about *that*?

Antony wanted to renew his alliance with Cleopatra, if not for love, then for money—hers. He needed her wealth if he was ever going to topple Octavian. Left, one of the many images of Cleopatra coined during her reign.

Antony—One Busy Guy

Antony seemed to like marriage. After all, he married five times!

We don't know much about his first two wives, but his third—Fulvia—was a strong and powerful woman. Cicero accused Antony of being the type of guy who would "rather obey a ... woman than the people of Rome." He meant that as an insult—and he was referring to Fulvia.

Antony had two sons with Fightin' Fulvia—Marcus Antonius Antyllus and Iullus Antonius. Fulvia failed in her attempt to overthrow Octavian, but it says a lot that she even tried! Many Romans dissed Fulvia for her strength and power in the same way they dissed Cleopatra. In different circumstances, these two powerful women might even have been kindred spirits.

Antony's fourth wife—Octavia—was more subtle, but also strong. She and Antony had two girls—both named Antonia (Antonia Major and Antonia Minor). Eventually, the girls reared three future Roman emperors (either as mothers or grandmothers)—Caligula, Claudius, and Nero, which meant three of the first five emperors of Rome were kin to Antony!

Cleopatra, Antony's fifth wife, eventually had three children by Antony. With seven children by three different moms, Antony appeared to be a very busy guy.

Antony claimed his family descended from Hercules (pictured), specifically his son Anton. Given his talent for marriage, he certainly seemed to have a Herculean appetite for strong women!

Love and Games 2.0

Was this an image of Cleopatra or of a Roman woman dressed up to look like her? We may never know. Antony, however, seemed never to doubt whom he could count on to achieve his goals—the Queen of Egypt.

ANTONY DISCOVERED THAT HIS POLITICAL
marriage to Octavia was like a lyre (an ancient stringed instrument). After the
pretty music was over, the strings were still attached. And those strings kept

The union of Octavia and Antony may have sounded like music to Rome's ears, but in the end, it all fell flat.

Antony tied up in knots. After all, he married Octavia to make peace with his enemy. But the only kind of peace Octavian wanted with Antony was one that included these initials: RIP, as in "Rest in Peace."

See, Octavian repeatedly reneged on the promises he made Antony when he convinced him to marry his sister. Antony finally accepted that Octavian never intended to support him or his war effort in Parthia. So he left for the East once again, leaving Octavia behind. As he had done years before, Antony sent for Cleopatra: *Meet me in Syria*, he commanded. He was ready to pick up where they had left off.

Cleopatra's response? We don't know exactly, but we can imagine it might have gone something like this:

Are you kidding me, fool?!

The queen wasn't about to be burned again. Yeah, she'd show up, and

yeah, she'd help him. But this time, instead of arriving on a golden boat filled with beautiful young women, she came with an agreement that would make even the toughest Hollywood lawyer proud. If Antony wanted Egypt's help again, she demanded that he:

- Marry her in a public ceremony. The marriage ceremony was a message to Rome—Egypt would not be Rome's mistress but a legitimate partner.

- Give up any hopes of ruling Egypt beside her. (Ouch!) That honor would go to her son Caesarion.

- Acknowledge their twins—Alexander Helios and Cleopatra Selene— as his own.

- Turn parts of Syria, Judea, and Arabia over to her, under Egyptian rule. Remember, Cleopatra was determined to strengthen and enlarge her kingdom to its former glory.

Antony was caught between a rock and a hard … pyramid. He couldn't go back to Rome after ditching his loyal Roman wife. But without Cleopatra's help, he couldn't move forward in his war, either. So he agreed to most of her terms.

Was he just caving in to Cleopatra's charms, as Octavian claimed? Not at all. Antony served his own ambitions. Ultimately, he wanted to be sole ruler of Rome. He figured conquering Parthia was the first step. But he needed a bigger navy, and Cleopatra promised to build him one. Egypt, however, had no trees and she needed wood to make boats. By putting forested regions in Syria and lands bordering Judea into Cleopatra's hands, Antony gave her the means to build up his navy.

But he didn't give Cleopatra *everything* she wanted—especially cities in Judea. Those he left with his henchman, King Herod. Still, giving away *any* Roman land horrified the Romans.

To them, it was as if Batman had turned over the Batmobile keys to the Joker. Only nobody was laughing.

The Romans frothed at the mouth. How dare a Roman leader give away Roman territory to a foreign ruler—let alone a *woman*?! And how could he agree to a marriage ceremony? Hello, wasn't he already married to the lovely Octavia?

Octavian must have rubbed his hands with glee at the opportunity to trash-talk his frenemy. He claimed Cleopatra bewitched Antony yet again. That Antony had lost his manhood. That the evil queen had strange powers of seduction that would make good Romans lose their minds, etc., etc.

Yet Antony, despite his good-ol'-boy charm, was a smart guy. He must have known his countrymen would howl at his decision to marry Cleopatra. So why risk it?

Rome Rage

Cleopatra was a sharp negotiator. Was she, perhaps, too sharp for Antony? Or did he deem her terms worthy of the risk? Either way, the Romans were furious with Antony.

He likely agreed to Cleopatra's terms because they seemed like a decent gamble. He probably figured Romans would forgive him pretty quickly once he came home a war hero. After all, conquering Parthia was something even the great Caesar hadn't accomplished. Defeating their longtime enemy would bring glory—not to mention added territory and riches—to the Roman Empire. Surely the Romans would push the pip-squeak Octavian off the podium and put Antony in charge after his victory.

Great idea. Only one problem. He actually had to *win* the war.

Cleopatra the ... Chaste?

The Roman West portrayed Cleopatra as an evil, vampy man-eater. Yet the Arab East—according to recent research on medieval Arabic writings—portrayed her as a "Virtuous Scholar."

Okay, wait. How can one person go from harlot to bookworm in one breath? What was it about Cleopatra that drove people to such extremes?

A Western Obsession

Rome downplayed Cleopatra's renowned brilliance by calling her names that insulted her moral character—especially when it came to relationships. Yet by ancient and modern standards, Cleopatra was chaste. She had only two romantic relationships her whole life. After Caesar, her first partner, died, there is no record of her being with anyone else—and you can bet people seriously watched her every move so they could gossip about her. She guarded the connection she had with Rome via her son Caesarion, whom she hoped would bridge the gap between the two powers.

When she married Antony, the insults came even more furiously. Yet Cleopatra proved faithful to Antony, refusing to betray him even when Octavian promised to spare her children—and her own life—if she killed him!

The queen proved her loyalty. But you wouldn't guess that from Octavian's propaganda!

Medieval Arab scholars painted an entirely different picture of the last pharaoh of Egypt. Having deciphered hieroglyphics hundreds of years before Westerners, these scholars used original Egyptian sources to write about Cleopatra. And their take on the queen was shockingly different from the West's.

They described her as a "strong and able" monarch whose only interest was protecting Egypt. In fact, they called her an "Egyptian national heroine." They also claimed she was a great scholar who wrote books on math, alchemy (a form of early chemistry), and medicine and held regular seminars to mix it up with top scientists from different fields. They credited her with starting impressive building and canal projects and even with sponsoring a hydrological project that reclaimed land from the sea.

According to the East, Cleopatra was more of a thinker than a lover. So which version should we believe? The West's "Hollywood" version of a supervixen, or the East's image of a brilliant and serious bookworm?

Without Cleopatra's own writings, we'll never know the truth. Still, we can make up our own minds by looking at the motivations behind each image. In the West, Romans smeared Cleopatra's reputation to avoid the shame of almost losing a war to a woman. In the East, medieval Arabs—with no agenda for disparaging the queen—celebrated her as a philosopher-scholar of the highest order.

Each side had a particular view. Given that Cleopatra—like all of us—was an imperfect human being, it's a good bet that the truth lies somewhere in between.

Killer Plans

Nothing says romance quite like injury and death on the battlefield. Or so it seemed for the newly wed couple.

SO WHAT DID THE ROMANTIC NEWLYWEDS

do for their honeymoon? They planned a *war*. Because, you know, nothin' says lovin' quite like dead bodies on the battlefield.

The now officially married Antony and Cleopatra planned to attack Rome's enemy—Parthia (ancient Iraq-Iran)—by marching through Armenia. But some wondered, was Armenia on their side? Oh yeah, Antony claimed. Absolutely.

So the bride gave Antony a fleet of ships. Her navy in the Mediterranean would hug the coast, covering his army's rear. That was the plan, anyway.

Cleopatra's Campaign

After Antony left for Armenia, Cleopatra went on her own campaign. But this one involved smiles, not swords. Remember the territories in Syria near Judea that Antony gave her? Cleopatra strengthened her hold on them with a public relations tour of duty. Pregnant with their third child (her fourth), the queen reveled in her new territories. And it appears her new citizens welcomed her with open arms.

Meanwhile, Antony entered Armenia on his march to Parthia. But to his shock, angry Armenian soldiers swarmed his army like paparazzi on a Hollywood movie star. The Armenian king had double-crossed him.

Fending off the unexpected aggression left Antony's army open to attack. That's when the Parthians stormed in, demolishing Antony's forces. Antony scurried out of Armenia faster than a Rollerblader careening downhill. Not only had he failed to conquer Parthia, but a former ally had betrayed him. The so-called conquering hero barely made it out alive.

"Oops, I Lost the War!"

While Antony faced a rout, Cleopatra gave birth to their son Ptolemy Philadelphus. Soon after, she received a message from Antony, this time from Beirut: *Help!*

Antony had lost half his forces. He and his army—what was left of it, anyway—were starving. They wouldn't make it through the winter without her aid. Cleopatra came to the rescue, but it took some time for her to arrive. While he waited, Antony began drinking heavily.

Octavian jumped on Antony's misfortune faster than a starving dog on a juicy bone. And—surprise, surprise—he blamed Cleopatra for everything: Antony couldn't think straight because he was besotted with Cleopatra, Octavian claimed. The truth? Antony had not adequately secured Armenia before going on the attack—a serious tactical error.

Cleopatra delayed helping Antony because she was looking for a way to betray him, Octavian accused. The truth? Her generals were in charge of organizing the support, and it was a huge effort. Also Cleopatra delivered, as promised.

Still, Antony's setback was just the excuse Octavian needed to pump up the volume on his anti-Cleopatra rant. And this time the whole world listened.

Octavian's Epic Plan

To redeem himself, Antony needed more Roman soldiers. Antony hadn't forgotten the men Octavian had promised him. He demanded that Octavian finally pay up.

Antony pressed him: deliver the 20,000 soldiers you promised me, man! Octavian's response? Okay, sure, no problem. Only somehow, he "forgot" a zero. He sent 2,000 soldiers, instead of 20,000!

Antony lost it. What an insult! How dare Octavian diss him like that. A promise was a promise! And to make matters worse, Octavia—Antony's Roman wife—insisted on coming along with the soldiers. In a rage, Antony sent her back to Rome.

Octavian must have danced a little jig of victory. See, the minute Antony rejected Octavia, it was as if he had copped to being a "bad" Roman. Octavian forced Antony to choose between his "sweet, good" Roman wife and the "evil seductress" Cleopatra.

Talk about a genius trap. On the one hand, if Antony had gone back to Rome with Octavia, he would've been admitting that he couldn't cut it on his own. Octavian would've won. On the other, by choosing Cleopatra, it looked as if he had gone over to the dark side and abandoned Rome, which meant Octavian won there, too.

Antony had been outfoxed.

Hittin' the Road

All roads didn't just "lead to Rome," they also led out of it. And usually by the thousands in marching formation. The roads moved Roman armies around the Empire quickly.

With instant messaging, cell phones, and e-mail, it's hard to imagine the slow pace of ancient communications. When Antony in Alexandria wrote to Octavian in Rome, the letter likely traveled by donkey or horse, carriage, and ship. Delivery took anywhere from a matter of weeks if they were lucky, to a matter of months if they were not.

See, everything depended on the season. The seas "closed" for the winter, because storms made it too dangerous for most ships to make the crossing. When the seas were "open," pirates and shipwrecks usually meant trouble. It wasn't much better on land, either. What if somebody filched your filly? Or jumped your messenger? So many things could go wrong it's a wonder any letters made it through at all.

Messages from rulers like Antony and Octavian got through quicker, though, because they used military messengers. Nothing like a guy with a shiny sword to make things move faster!

Later, Octavian instituted a system—much like the early Pony Express— where messengers on official government business relied on special relay stations ready with fresh horses. The Romans called this the *cursus publicus*. This "public course," though, was only for government communications. If you wanted to send a personal letter, you had to find—and pay—your own way.

Rome eventually built a network of roads that spanned close to fifty thousand miles, all designed to move Roman legions into every corner of the empire. Octavian, later called Augustus, initiated this great network of roads, which also helped speed communications around the empire.

Rome sat in the center of the great hub. The Romans continued building roads for centuries. And when the last road was finished, can you guess how they cut the opening-day ribbon? With a pair of Caesars, of course!

"I'll Scratch Your Back if You Scratch Mine"

It was clear that Antony had no future without Cleopatra. But Cleopatra had her own agenda. Remember, she was determined to restore her kingdom to the glory days of Egypt. And that meant territory. If he needed more help from her, then she would get more land from him.

This time, Antony gave her portions of Judea. King Herod was furious but powerless to stop the deal. The Romans also howled in protest. How dare he give away even more Roman-owned property? But what could Antony do? Without the promised soldiers from Octavian, Antony had no choice but to rely on Cleopatra.

So the queen financed his second effort into Armenia. Fortunately, he won. Antony captured the double-crossing Armenian king but didn't advance into Parthia. Yet. He still had the continuing problem of not having enough Roman soldiers.

Still, a victory was a victory. Antony desperately needed a positive spin on recent events. He hoped to have Rome eating out of his hands. After all, Romans adored a winning general. But what he did next had them throwing up their hands in disgust instead.

A Triumphant Misstep

To celebrate a war victory, Romans held what they called a triumph. Think of it as an ego pageant. The victorious general paraded through the streets of Rome, showing off what he stole … er, won … from the country he invaded. The Romans loved their triumphs. Not just because it felt good to see themselves as masters of the world, but also because the government usually paid for the food and wine. Party time! The celebrations could last for days. The partying even had a religious vibe, because the conquering hero was likened to a god.

So what did Antony do that had everybody in Rome gasping in horror? Drum roll, please: Antony held his triumph not in Rome but in Alexandria, Egypt.

It came down to this: the Romans flew into a fury about having their party taken out of their city.

The Romans took their right to party seriously. Here a Roman emperor who ruled almost one hundred years after Antony enters the city for his sacred parade.

The Horror! The Horror!

To be fair, imagine if the Super Bowl moved to China without warning, or if the World Series showed up in France. Enraged Americans would demand the head of the person in charge, which is pretty much what happened to Antony.

But Antony made things even worse. At his triumph, he shared his spoils of war—not with Rome but with his Egyptian family. In what historians call the "Donations of Alexandria," Antony gave Libya and Syria to Cleopatra. He named their six-year-old son, Alexander Helios, the new king of Armenia (the country that dared defeat him earlier). The boy's twin, Cleopatra Selene, got

Cyrenaica and parts of Crete, and the two-year-old, Ptolemy Philadelphus, got Phoenicia, Syria, and Cilicia.

Imagine the outrage if the vice president of the United States suddenly gave away parts of Alaska, or the governor-general of Canada donated Nova Scotia to another country without permission. Had Antony lost his mind?

Octavian leaped at Antony's public relations disaster. He called Antony anti-Roman, and he claimed that Antony even planned to move the capital of Rome to Egypt. Worse, Octavian claimed Antony's behavior wasn't even his fault. An evil force was using him as a puppet. That force had to be stopped—not just for Antony's protection but also for Rome's.

That horrible and dangerous evil force? You guessed it: the queen of Egypt—Cleopatra. Never mind that Antony was a big boy and had made his own political decisions for decades. Never mind that his strategy—okay, gamble—for power was one that he himself had chosen. It *had* to be the woman's fault.

Cleopatra became the symbol for the destructive power of the East, which Romans associated with Egypt. A power that the "good Roman" Octavian was ready to stamp out.

But not, Cleopatra swore, without one heck of a fight.

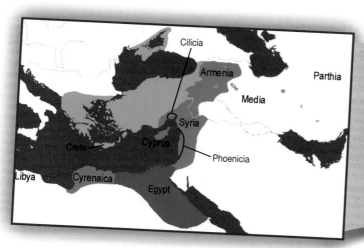

Plutarch dubbed Antony's land gifts to his Egyptian family the "Donations of Alexandria." Octavian called it cuckoo. Antony named Cleopatra and Caesarion rulers of Egypt, Libya, and Cyprus. To Alexander Helios, he gave Armenia and Parthia (not yet conquered). Cleopatra Selene got Crete and Cyrenaica, while the toddler Ptolemy Philadelphus got Phoenicia, Syria, and Cilicia.

Disaster near the Delta

Octavian would soon drown all of Antony and Cleopatra's hopes.

OCTAVIAN DECLARED WAR—NOT ON ANTONY

but on Cleopatra. This way, he could start a civil war without it *seeming* like a civil war. Smooth, right? The guy was more slippery than a guppy in Jell-O.

Still, declaring war on Cleopatra was a risky move. Octavian was actually in no position to fight. He was low on cash, his army wasn't ready, and Roman citizens raged at having to finance yet another war.

So why declare war? Because Antony gave him another opening. In the middle of Octavian's anti-Antony propaganda war, Antony divorced Octavian's sister Octavia. How? By kicking her out of his house (that's how ancient Roman men divorced their wives). Octavian wanted to milk the insult to his sister for all it was worth.

It was just too perfect. See, by divorcing his good Roman wife and staying with his Egyptian one, it was as if he "divorced' his own Romanness. Or, at least, that's what Octavian claimed.

Yet despite all the bad press, Antony still had a lot of Roman support in his corner. Most Romans, in fact, preferred Antony's fun-loving personality to Octavian's cold, slithery one. Some Romans even begged Antony to attack. Get Octavian now while he's weak, they prompted.

But Antony didn't attack. Why?

Nobody knows. Maybe Antony didn't like the idea of attacking his homeland. Or maybe he worried that Octavian was stronger than he was letting on. Either way, Antony avoided Rome. He didn't want Octavian coming to Egypt, though. So he headed for what he figured was neutral ground—Greece—to plan his and Cleopatra's defense. People wondered if Antony had lost his military mojo. Why was the right-hand man of the great Caesar playing defense instead of offense? Where had his gumption gone?

Antony had read the situation wrong once again. His delay gave Octavian the time he needed to strengthen his forces. It marked the beginning of the end for Antony and Cleopatra.

Greece Is the Word

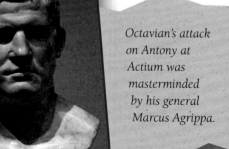

Octavian's attack on Antony at Actium was masterminded by his general Marcus Agrippa.

Cleopatra gave Antony two hundred warships to defend the coast during their Greek getaway. They anticipated a naval attack. Octavian's general Agrippa and his

Archaeologists have brought up artifacts near Actium they believe are remnants from the naval skirmish between Antony and Octavian. Bronze prow of a Roman ship.

navy blocked them by sea. Then Octavian and his forces approached on land, trapping the pair in a port city called Actium.

Octavian determined to starve them out. Months wore on, and Antony's supplies of water and food dwindled. Sickness spread. Hordes of Antony's soldiers defected to Octavian's side, breaking Antony's heart. How could they turn on him like that?

Antony and Cleopatra had to do something. And fast. That's when they made their escape. But not before one of Antony's key commanders scurried to Octavian's side and spilled their plans. Still, in a fierce naval engagement, Cleopatra's boat broke through Octavian's blockade. Antony brought up the rear. They'd done it. They'd made it out alive, but at a huge cost. They had managed a tactical victory—by escaping—but lost the war when most of Antony's forces defected to Octavian.

Octavian prompted those defections by trash-talking Antony worse than the second-place team at the cheerleading finals. Antony abandoned his men in his pitiful obsession with Cleopatra, he claimed. Focusing on Antony's supposed "lovesickness" distracted Roman soldiers from the fact that Cleopatra succeeded in breaking through Octavian's blockade in an unexpected and brilliant maneuver—one that left her and Antony alive to fight another day.

Instead, Octavian spread the message to Antony's land forces that Antony would abandon them for the queen. Huge numbers of men defected. Antony and Cleopatra had virtually no army left. As a result, they had no future either.

But you didn't dare tell Cleopatra that!

Cleopatra through the Ages

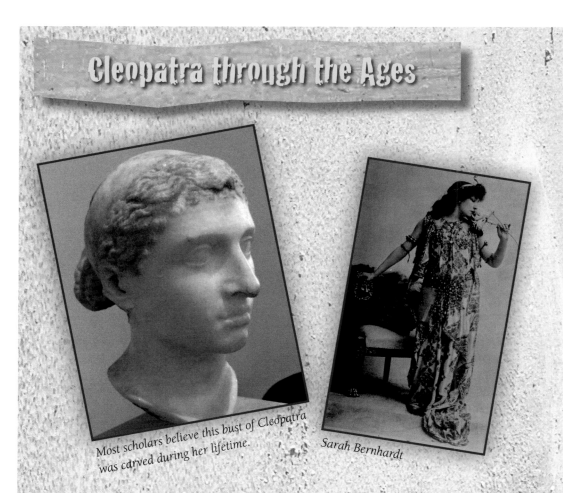

Most scholars believe this bust of Cleopatra was carved during her lifetime.

Sarah Bernhardt

Artists throughout history have tried to capture Cleopatra's supposedly "dangerous" beauty. But more often than not, they simply projected whatever beauty ideals were popular at the time.

For example, the ancient bust on the left was created during Cleopatra's own lifetime, giving us what we can assume was a fairly accurate representation of the great queen's looks.

During the Renaissance, artists often painted Cleopatra as a fair-skinned, light-eyed, voluptuous blond. In Hollywood, casting directors often chose fair-skinned, light-eyed sex symbols to play the queen. The trend shifted again in 2008, when a British Broadcasting Corporation (BBC) documentary depicted Cleopatra as a woman with cornrows and very dark skin.

Elizabeth Taylor

Ruth St. Denis

Computer-generated image created in 2008.

Claudette Colbert

From blond to dark, the images of Cleopatra have changed with the times and will likely continue to change. Still, there's one fact all scholars agree on—her nationality. Cleopatra was Greek (Macedonian). She came from a long line of Greek Ptolemies who intermarried within their own Greek bloodline. We've even got a letter of Cleopatra's that she signed in Greek! (See page 19.)

Cleopatra most likely had the olive skin, brown eyes, and black hair typical of her Mediterranean heritage. But again, as Plutarch noted, it wasn't necessarily her beauty that bewitched—it was the force of her personality and intelligence.

Death of a Pharaoh

Cleopatra's death was as dramatic as her life.

AFTER HER ESCAPE AT ACTIUM, CLEOPATRA

raced to Alexandria like a kid busting out of school on the last day. She had no time to lose. She worried that her enemies at the palace would take advantage of her weakness. The last thing she needed now was an attempt to overthrow her at home.

The always outrageous Cleopatra tried to haul her fleet over the desert to escape with her children via the Red Sea. Too bad it all went up in flames.

So Cleopatra created her own spin on the situation. She decorated her boat with garlands and had her musicians perform victory songs from the prow. Her ship must have looked like the winning float at a Super Bowl championship parade. Only it was the losing team claiming victory.

From the get-go, Antony moped over his losses—especially the defection of his men. It cut him deeply that the men he loved and fought with for years had so quickly turned on him.

But feisty Cleopatra refused to lose focus—or quit. Luckily, Octavian gave her plenty of time to come up with a plan. While he stayed near Greece strong-arming Antony's former allies, she came up with an outrageous scheme: she would move her fleet into the Red Sea and hightail it out of Egypt, hoping to get herself and her family to safety. They couldn't sail the Mediterranean—Octavian's navy already "owned" it. So she had her fleet hauled over the desert for a shortcut to the Red Sea. Pro-Octavian allies in Arabia, however, intercepted the boats and set them on fire. Cleopatra's plan to escape went up in smoke.

Request Denied

Antony, in the meantime, discovered that the land forces he had left in Libya—which he had planned to use in another strike—had also defected to Octavian. Now he had no army *or* navy—especially after the destruction of

Cleopatra's fleet. Antony could either surrender or head back to Cleopatra in Alexandria.

He headed back.

All of Antony's allies defected to Octavian, too, including Herod in Judea. Antony and Cleopatra were alone. So the lovers reunited. They knew they were doomed, so they started another club. Remember their "society" devoted to living the high life? Well, they started a new one, only this one was called The Order of the Inseparable in Death. The goal was to live it up with feasts and parties. They knew their time was running out. They might as well go out in style!

Meanwhile, despite all of the defections from Antony's camp, Octavian faced a tricky situation. Many soldiers hated the idea of fighting Antony—their former general whom they had loved and revered. Only one thing seemed to soothe their guilt—money, and lots of it.

But where could Octavian get his greedy hands on fast cash?

Like a cartoon character with dollar signs shining in his eyes, Octavian looked toward Cleopatra's fabled personal treasure. It was time to go after the queen in Alexandria.

"Save My Children, Please!"

As O-man and his forces advanced on Alexandria, Cleopatra sent a message: Spare my children. Let them inherit my kingdom.

And what would happen to her if he agreed? She didn't say. It was almost as if she were trading her life for her family.

One Roman historian claimed that Octavian sent a private response to the queen: kill Antony (or kick him to the curb) for me and I will pardon you and let you keep your throne.

The queen refused.

Yes, Cleopatra *refused* to betray Antony. So why has she always been depicted—from Shakespeare to George Bernard Shaw—as such a backstabbing double-crosser?

Cleopatra proved her loyalty to Antony, even when it was clear it would cost her everything, including control over her beloved country. Despite what Octavian had claimed, Cleopatra had her man's back.

© Ziad Nour

Out of all the images of Cleopatra we've seen over the centuries, few if any depict her as the devoted mom of four kids. Yet from the moment Cleopatra knew she could not escape, she negotiated furiously to save her children's lives.

Antony made one final attempt to stop Octavian in a battle in Alexandria. But all his remaining forces—including his cavalry—defected to Octavian's side. Every Roman abandoned him. When Cleopatra received the news of Antony's defeat by abandonment, she locked herself in her mausoleum (a large, temple-like building for housing her mummy after her death). Inside, she had earlier placed most of her royal treasure—including gold, silver, emeralds, pearls, ebony, ivory, and cinnamon—over a huge pyre, ready for torching. She knew Octavian wanted her wealth. Threatening to burn it gave her some negotiating power.

Meanwhile, Alexandria deteriorated into chaos. Rumors ran rampant. Antony learned—allegedly through a note from Cleopatra's servant—that the queen had committed suicide. He had lost everything.

Without checking for the truth, Antony pulled out his sword and begged his servant to kill him. The servant refused, killing himself instead. Antony then took the sword and stabbed himself in the belly. That's when another of Cleopatra's servants burst in.

Wait! The note was false.

Cleopatra lived.

Death of a Warrior

Antony wanted one last wish: to see Cleopatra before he died. Bleeding and gasping in pain, servants brought him to Cleopatra's mausoleum. But they couldn't get in. Cleopatra had barred the door for protection against Octavian's soldiers. Only Cleopatra and two female servants remained inside.

Unable or unwilling to unbar the door and risk capture, the queen and her servants used ropes and pulleys to bring up the barely conscious Antony through a second-story window. As soon as Cleopatra saw the dying Antony, she threw herself on him. In anguish, she called Antony her "lord, her husband." Antony begged her to save her own life.

Then died in her arms.

Cleopatra and Antony's two-for-one tomb was likely decorated like this one from the glory days of ancient Egypt, 1,200 years before Cleopatra's reign.

Octavian Closes In

Afraid that Cleopatra would commit suicide and torch the treasure he wanted so badly, Octavian sent his men to her mausoleum with a single order: bring her back alive.

Through the barred front door, one of his men negotiated with Cleopatra for the safety of her children. Meanwhile, another man used a ladder to sneak into the second-story window that Cleopatra had used to haul Antony inside. As the soldier approached her from behind, one of her ladies cried out in warning. Cleopatra grabbed a dagger hidden in her dress and tried to stab herself, but Octavian's man was too quick. She'd been captured. She was placed under guard with strict instructions to keep her alive.

Despondent and soon sick with fever, Cleopatra refused to eat. Octavian, worried that her behavior was a slow form of suicide, threatened to kill her children unless she took nourishment. So she ate.

In fact, Octavian threatened her children so often that one ancient historian said it was as if he attacked her with "engines of war"—something like emotional battering rams—to take her down. Yet she never gave up negotiating for their safety. She had already sent sixteen-year-old Caesarion away to India, hoping he'd survive there. Of all her children, he was the most vulnerable. With Caesar's blood in his veins, her teenage son was the biggest threat to the power-obsessed Octavian.

"I'll Make You Pay!"

Cleopatra learned that Octavian planned to take her and her remaining children to Rome. That could mean only one thing: he intended to parade her in chains in his triumph.

 92

Cleopatra would not let him have the satisfaction. Now a prisoner in the palace, she asked permission to pray at Antony's tomb, which just happened to be in her mausoleum. What could Octavian say to such an innocent request? He let her go, accompanied by two of her most loyal ladies-in-waiting.

When she finished her ritual prayers at Antony's tomb, she sent a note to Octavian, then closed the doors to the tomb for privacy. The letter contained only one request: to be buried next to Antony.

Octavian jumped in alarm—this could mean only one thing. She was going to commit suicide. He sent his soldiers racing to the mausoleum to stop her.

Her Final Victory

Meanwhile, an Egyptian peasant brought a basket of figs for the grieving queen. The guards outside the building—not suspecting a thing—let the gift through. But the basket hid a secret. Underneath the ripe fruit slithered the means for Cleopatra's final "escape"—an Egyptian cobra, also called an asp.

Reclining on a golden couch, the queen reached for the snake. It sprang out and struck.

Octavian's messengers burst through the door to find the queen apparently asleep. *She's dead,* one of the queen's ladies—also dying— told them. And, with her last breath, added, "It was a death fitting for one descended from so many kings."

Octavian's men tried to revive the queen, but it was over. The last pharaoh of Egypt was gone.

According to Plutarch, Cleopatra was devastated at the loss of her beloved Antony, who died in her arms.

11

From the moment of her death, Cleopatra became an instant celebrity.

CLEOPATRA'S SPECTACULAR DEATH MADE HER an instant celebrity. After all, here was a proud and powerful woman who said, "I will not give my enemies the satisfaction of killing me. I will do it myself." And then reached for a hissing snake.

 94

Or did she?

No one knows for sure whether a snake's hiss was the last sound Cleopatra heard. Yet when it came to showing off at his triumph in Rome, Octavian paraded a statue of Cleopatra in her death throes, attached to a snake. True or not, the image sunk its teeth into myth and never let go.

Scholars still argue about the snake. Some claim she died of poison. Others say the snake death made the most sense. After all, death by snake venom is a relatively painless way to go. Egyptians often used the bite of a cobra to carry out the death penalty. The Egyptian cobra served as an important royal symbol. And Cleopatra rocked *three* snakes (called uraei) on her royal headdress, instead of the typical single snake (uraeus).

Cleopatra knew how to make a spectacular entrance. It seemed fitting that she would opt for snakes to create the most dramatic exit, too.

Cleopatra rocked three snakes, called uraei, on her crown. Uraeus is a Greek word derived from an Egyptian word meaning "rearing cobra."

Are You My Mummy?

Where is Cleopatra's mummy? Sadly, the secret of her final resting place remains under wraps.

Many believe Cleopatra's tomb lies somewhere deep under the streets of modern Alexandria. Since Cleopatra was entombed alongside Antony, according to her last wish, the archaeologist who discovers her burial place will likely get a "two-for-one" deal.

Although the glory days of mummification peaked thousands of years before Cleopatra, the practice continued until Christianity spread throughout Egypt (around the fourth century CE). For most of Egypt's history, mummification was the ticket to an endless life.

Major Mummies

The mummification process took about seventy days. But the results, the Egyptians believed, lasted for eternity.

Egyptians believed that a soul without a body was like a hot dog without a bun. You needed one to enjoy the other. Over thousands of years, they experimented with many techniques for preserving bodies. In the early stages, they tried wrapping the body in resin-coated linen. That worked fine on the outside, but the body parts on the inside melted into a stinky mess.

Eventually, they perfected the process by cutting into the lower abdomen and removing most of the major organs, then packing the body in

Ever hear someone say their heart is heavy? It might be a holdover from ancient Egyptian times when a too-heavy heart—one that weighed more than the Feather of Truth—caused you to fail the judgment of Anubis and condemned you to an eternity of misery.

natron, a type of salt used for drying. The organs, stuffed into special jars, stayed near the body. They pulled the brains out through the nose. After all, who needed brains? The ancient Egyptians thought they were worthless.

Meanwhile, the heart was often left untouched inside the body. Why? Because you needed your heart for the special weigh-in against the Feather of Truth. If your heart passed the test (weighed less than the feather), then you entered the afterworld. If it didn't, a crocodile-headed monster gobbled up your heart—along with your chances for making it into the afterworld.

Once the body dried, the priests rubbed it with sacred oils, and then wrapped it. The embalmers often placed sacred amulets throughout the wrappings for protection. They considered these amulets lucky charms. Too bad so many tomb robbers were magically malicious. They stole countless amulets and charms, unwrapping and destroying mummies along the way.

Kings, queens, and other powerful folk put their tombs deep underground for safekeeping. During the Ptolemaic era (when Cleopatra's family ruled), people who couldn't afford tombs kept mummies at home. Sometimes they'd stick 'em in a corner, sometimes in front of a special shrine. Ancient kids didn't always show respect for their elders. Sometimes they scribbled all over the cases. They probably got in big trouble for defacing their ancestors.

Which is why we can guess that at least one of them must have said, "Please, don't tell mummy!"

What Happened to Cleopatra's Kids

Cleopatra's teenage son, Caesarion (right), had ruled alongside her for years. Cleopatra tried to save his life by sending him to India, but Octavian had him hunted down and murdered.

Poor Caesarion. The sixteen-year-old son of Caesar and Cleopatra almost made it. Remember, his mother had sent him to India, hoping he could hide out there for a while. But on the way there, his tutor double-crossed him. Secretly working for Octavian, the tutor told the boy that he should go back. Caesarion hesitated. *Octavian wants you to rule in your mother's place,* he claimed. Like his mother, Caesarion couldn't turn his back on his country. He headed back to Egypt. Octavian's men hunted him down and killed him.

Cleopatra's children by Antony—Alexander Helios, Cleopatra Selene (both ten years old), and Ptolemy Philadelphus (almost six)—were shipped off to Rome.

Octavian paraded them in his triumph. They walked in gold chains, trailing a rendering of their mother dying by the bite of a snake. Octavian then handed Cleopatra's kids over to Octavia—Antony's ex-wife—his own sister. She raised them alongside her own girls by Antony and Antony's other son by Fulvia. When Cleopatra Selene was fifteen, she was married off to King Juba II, the African king of Mauretania (today's Morocco and Algeria). Many scholars think her twin and younger brother died during their stay in Rome.

Cleopatra's youngest son, Ptolemy Philadelphus, was named after Ptolemy II, who completed the construction of the Great Library.

© Kathleen Cohen

The only child of Cleopatra's that survived the Roman defeat was her daughter, Cleopatra VIII Selene. She grew up to rule in North Africa as Queen of Mauretania.

© Mary Harrsch

Ptolemy of Mauretania, son of Cleopatra Selene and Juba II, was the only known grandchild of the great queen. Ptolemy ruled as king in Mauretania but was killed in 40 CE by the Roman Emperor Caligula (also a descendant of Ptolemy's grandfather, Mark Antony). Why? Because Cleopatra's grandson wore a purple cloak that was prettier than his own.

Octavian, renamed Augustus, slowly took control of the entire government and became Rome's first emperor.

After Cleopatra's death, Octavian took her treasure and melted down the gold and silver to pay his soldiers. Then he annexed Egypt, turning it into his own personal, private estate. If Roman citizens wanted to visit "his" Egypt, they had to ask for special permission. In addition to plundering its riches, Octavian controlled the region by appointing only low-ranking, fiercely loyal Romans to manage it for him. He never risked putting a strong general or politician in charge, fearing that an ambitious man could hijack Egypt's wealth to challenge him for control of the empire. Cleopatra's dream of a strong and independent Egypt drifted away like sand in the desert wind.

Later, the Senate changed Octavian's name to Augustus, which meant "sacred" or "revered." Then they renamed the month in which he defeated Cleopatra—Sextilis—after him, to August. Octavian also named August 1 as a holiday to celebrate his victory over Egypt.

Augustus proved to be a brilliant administrator. He stabilized Rome and increased its territories. He used the wealth of Egypt to strengthen Rome's infrastructure—its impressive roads, public buildings, and aqueducts. He lived forty-four years after Cleopatra and wrote (or rewrote, depending on your view) her history.

"Liar, Liar, Pants on Fire"

Since Octavian-Augustus lived for decades after Cleopatra, he had plenty of time to mess with her image so that she came out looking like a witch—while he ended up looking like a superhero. Just look at how he manipulated the facts.

- Despite relying on his own wife for counsel, Octavian acted as if it were a crime that Antony treated Cleopatra as an equal. Instead, he promoted the traditional Roman belief that women should stay in the home and not involve themselves in politics. He even claimed that Cleopatra was "unnatural" because she was brilliant and powerful.

- Instead of holding Antony accountable for his actions, Octavian blamed Cleopatra for everything. This way, he would not appear to attack a fellow Roman in a mad grab for power, though that was exactly what he had done.

- Octavian claimed that Cleopatra wanted to conquer Rome and make all Romans her slaves. Not true. What Cleopatra really wanted, most scholars now say, was to strengthen her kingdom and act as Rome's partner in the East.

- Cleopatra and Antony escaped at Actium from a seemingly inescapable naval blockade. Octavian made it sound as if Cleopatra abandoned Antony and that lovesick Antony, in turn, abandoned his men to chase after her. Most scholars now believe the escape from Actium was a well-coordinated effort. After all, the pair lived to fight again—and likely would have if Octavian hadn't so successfully trash-talked Antony. Massive defections from Antony's forces and allies defeated Antony more soundly than Actium did.

- Octavian argued that Antony's love for Cleopatra weakened him. But after defeating him, he made Antony seem like a vicious, bloodthirsty warrior. Why? So he could seem more like a stud for stopping him. But Octavian barely even fought! His general Agrippa masterminded all military efforts.

- Octavian claimed to have discovered Antony's will, alleging that Antony planned, among other outrages, to move the capital of Rome to Egypt. Most scholars believe Octavian faked the contents of the will to whip Romans into an anti-Antony frenzy.

- Octavian maintained that Egyptians—especially the powerful priests—hated Cleopatra. But when he began destroying her statues after her death, Egyptian priests *begged* him to stop. They even gave Octavian a huge amount of money—enough to pay for his army for a *year*—as a bribe to keep him from continuing the destruction. Octavian took the priests' money—then destroyed most of her statues anyway.

Egyptian priests begged Octavian not to destroy Cleopatra's statues, but he ignored them. Another famous female pharaoh Hatshepsut (pictured) also had her statues destroyed.

Thanks to Octavian, we know Rome's point of view, but what did Egyptians think of Cleopatra? After Cleopatra died, the Egyptian priests, remember, paid Octavian-Augustus a large sum of money to keep her statues safe. They would not have done so if they had not respected her. Clearly, they wanted to honor her.

A weaving found in Koptos (the modern Egyptian city of Qift) and dated to about six months before Cleopatra's death, described her as "Mother of kings, queen of kings, youngest goddess." She was, to her people, Cleopatra-Isis, mother of kings and protector of her country.

Try as he might, that's one fact Octavian could never rewrite.

Chapter Endnotes

Chapter One

[1] Page 10—Shakespeare used Plutarch's biography of Mark Antony to write his tragic play on the famous couple. But most scholars believe Plutarch went heavy on drama and sometimes light on truth. And Shakespeare, no surprise, amped the drama. *Antony and Cleopatra,* act 1, scene 2, line 51.

[2] Page 10—At the Great Library of Alexandria, Cleopatra would likely have studied arithmetic, geometry, music, rhetoric, astronomy, science, and medicine, according to many scholars. She also would have studied—like her male counterparts—Egyptian history, Greek history, and Greek literature—in particular Homer (*The Iliad* and *The Odyssey*) and Greek poetry and drama. Jones, *Cleopatra,* pp. 19–20.

[3] Page 10—Not all scholars believe eleven-year-old Cleopatra accompanied her father on this trip to Rome. Grant, however, believes she did, citing a marker in Athens (a stopover on the way) honoring the death of a princess's lady-in-waiting from the region. Grant, *Cleopatra,* p. 15. Also, Grant seems to think that even the Piper wouldn't have been stupid enough to leave all three of his princesses alone under one roof while he was away! After all, when he got back, he had his oldest girl killed because she dared to take the throne. Jones, *Cleopatra,* p. 13. Kleiner also conjectures that Cleopatra accompanied Auletes, writing that she got to "see the world with her father." Kleiner, *Cleopatra and Rome,* p. 23.

[4] Page 11—The loan shark that loaned Auletes the huge sums of money was so worried about getting it back, he convinced Cleopatra's dad to put him in charge of all the finances in Alexandria. Then, when the greedy Roman squeezed them for payback too hard, Auletes was thrown out in a popular uprising. Dickson interview, 2008.

[5] Page 14—Besides Plutarch, other ancient Roman writers tell us their versions of events, including Caesar himself (before he got murdered, that is) as well as Suetonius, Dio, and others. Dickson points out that "All of these sources were written fifty-plus years after the events and were written to moralize and reinforce Roman stereotypes—especially as they related to women." Interview, 2008.

[6] Page 15—Plutarch wrote that the "rulers of Egypt before her had never even troubled to learn the Egyptian language. . . . " *Makers of Rome,* "Mark Antony," 27.21. However, most scholars have a hard time believing that she was the only one of *all* the Ptolemies to learn Egyptian. She was certainly the last to do so! Plutarch also claimed that she could easily converse with "Ethiopians, Troglodytes, Hebrews, Arabians, Syrians, Medes, or Parthians." 27.3.

[7] Page 16—Cleopatra had to rule with her brother, according to Daddy's will. Caesar in *The Civil War,* wrote, "One copy of the will had been taken to Rome by his emissaries to be placed in the treasury, but since, owing to the political troubles, this had proved impossible, the will had been deposited instead with Pompey." *The Civil War,* "The Alexandrian War," 108.15.

104

[8] Page 18—A marker of the period records that Cleopatra was present at the ceremony for the new Buchis bull and that "all the people saw her." Another stele shows that within a year after her ascension, Cleopatra donated a large sum of money for the upkeep for the recently deceased Apis bull—another sacred bull cult. Hamer, *Signs of Cleopatra,* p. 14.

[9] Page 18—Tyldesley says the Buchis bull "received offerings, delivered oracles and cured the sick (specializing in eye diseases). . . ." Sometimes they even fought other bulls in special bullrings. *Cleopatra: Last Queen of Egypt,* p. 41.

Chapter Two

[1] Page 24—According to Plutarch, the mini-king's advisers worried that if they welcomed Pompey, Caesar would get mad. But if they made him leave, both leaders would be furious—Pompey at the insult and Caesar at the continued chase! So the decision was made: "Kill him." Soon after, Pompey fell head over heels. Literally. Plutarch, *Fall of the Roman Republic,* "Pompey," 77.14

[2] Page 25—Plutarch, in the *Fall of the Roman Republic,* claimed that Caesar "secretly sent for" Cleopatra. The servant who snuck her in was Apollodorus. Plutarch also claimed that she rolled herself in a sleeping bag, not a rug. "Caesar," 49.6.

[3] Page 26—Plutarch claimed her voice was lovely too—that it was "a delight merely to hear the sound of her voice. . . ." Thanks to Hollywood, though, it's hard to picture Cleopatra as only mildly attractive. We tend to picture her as a knock-out. *Makers of Rome,* "Antony," 27.14.

[4] Page 28—Caesar actually gave Cyprus to Cleopatra's youngest brother, Ptolemy XIV, and Arsinoe IV, according to one historian (Jones, *Cleopatra,* p. 33). Whether it was given in name only is not clear. He was likely throwing the Egyptians a bone to keep them off Cleopatra's back. It didn't work. Kleiner, *Cleopatra and Rome,* p. 79.

Chapter Three

[1] Page 33—Most scholars think it was the library warehouse—and not the great Library—that Caesar torched. Either way, it's likely that many irreplaceable scrolls were lost. Jones, *Cleopatra,* p. 36.

[2] Page 33—Caesar wrote that he sent small boats out to rescue the men he left when he jumped ship. Funny fact: Caesar wrote about himself in the third person! *The Civil War,* "Alexandria," 21.9, p. 178.

[3] Page 35— (caption). Chauveau claims Antony's "plunder of the library at Pergamon" was designed to make up for the loss of books after Caesar burnt the scroll warehouse in Alexandria years before. *Egypt in the Age of Cleopatra,* p. 61.

[4] Page 35—Cleopatra rebuilt the library/warehouse Caesar burned down. But the library itself eventually burned down completely centuries later. Modern Egyptians have built a new Alexandrian library on the site of Cleopatra's palace. Like its ancient predecessor, the library houses a museum and planetarium. Check it out at http://www.bibalex.org/English/index.aspx.

[5] Page 37—To appease sticklers for tradition, Cleopatra named her youngest brother as co-ruler. But he really wasn't. He was too young to have any advisers so she had

nothing to worry about. She ruled all. Years later, the boy would die—some say of sickness; others accused the queen of killing him.

[6] Page 39—Cleopatra's ancestor Ptolemy II paid for the lighthouse and demanded his name carved on it. But the architect, Sostratus, wanted some of the credit too. So, according to legend, he played a little trick on the pharaoh. He chiseled his own name in stone and then covered it up with plaster. On the plaster, he carved the Pharaoh's name. Over the years, the plaster wore away, leaving the architect's name for all to see! Pollard, *The Rise and Fall of Alexandria,* p. 91.

[7] page 39—The Seven Wonders of the Ancient World include the Great Pyramid of Giza, the Hanging Gardens of Babylon, the Temple of Artemis at Epheus, the Colossus of Rhodes, the Mausoleum at Halicarnassus, and the Lighthouse of Alexandria.

Chapter Four

[1] Page 37—The Romans never allowed foreign rulers to reside within the city limits of Rome. It's a good thing Caesar had the lovely villa across the Tiber. Where else would Cleopatra have stayed? Certainly not in his house with his Roman wife!

[2] Page 44—The Greek historian Herodotus visited Egypt in the fifth century BCE. He pointed out that if a cat was killed by accident (rather than on purpose), the punishment was a fine, not death. But if an ibis or hawk was killed—accident or no—the punishment was always death. *Histories,* 2.67.

[3] Page 45—When Cleopatra visited Cyprus in 44 BCE, after Caesar's assassination, she restored her authority over the island without question. Bronze coins of the period show Cleopatra holding a newborn Caesarion in her arms. Chauveau, *Cleopatra Beyond the Myth,* p. 33.

[4] Page 45—After checking on Cyprus, Cleopatra concentrated on keeping Egypt stable during the upheaval in Rome. Her coruler, the then-teenage Ptolemy XIV, died soon after. Some ancient writers, such as Josephus, claimed she had him killed, though others believed he became sick and died. Kleiner, *Cleopatra and Rome,* p. 91. Josephus also claimed that she had little sister Arsinoe killed. Josephus, *The Works of Flavius Josephus: Antiquities of the Jews,* Book 15, 4.1

[5] Page 46—Cicero wrote "I can't stand the queen. . . ." She promised him "all things of the learned sort . . ." Cicero also claimed he hated the "Queen's insolence, too, when she was living in Caesar's trans-Tiberine villa" and that he couldn't even think about her "without a pang." *Letters,* XXXII.

[6] Page 48—The empire was split in three among Octavian, Antony, and Lepidus. But Lepidus wasn't a real player or threat. The real power struggle was between Octavian and Antony.

Chapter Five

[1] Page 50—The accusation of having a hand in Caesar's death must have rankled the young queen (as well as made her fear for her life). Caesar's assassination was a political nightmare for Cleopatra. She was so furious over his murder, she galvanized a fleet to go after his assassins—Cassius and Brutus—but never made it to the Battle of Philippi where Antony and Octavian defeated them. Kleiner, *Cleopatra and Rome,* p. 102.

[2] Page 50—Plutarch claimed Cleopatra arrived dressed as Venus (or Aphrodite, depending on the translation). Plutarch, *Makers of Rome,* "Antony," 26.4. The Egyptians, though, would have seen her as Isis. Jones claims that "it is likely . . . that she portrayed herself as Isis, whom Plutarch either understands or interprets for his Greek-speaking audience as Aphrodite." *Cleopatra,* p. 63. The ancients often saw other people's gods as different manifestations of their own gods; in this case, the Egyptian goddess of love—Isis—would have been described for Plutarch's audience as the Greek-Roman love goddess. But, according to Chauveau, it wasn't all just for show. "Isis was the omnipotent goddess of salvation," the French scholar writes. By associating herself with Isis, Cleopatra sent a message: she was determined to be the salvation of her nation. Chauveau, *Egypt in the Age of Cleopatra,* p. 110.

[3] Page 52—Plutarch's poetic description of Cleopatra's arrival has captivated the imagination of artists, writers, and moviemakers for centuries. Plutarch, *Makers of Rome,* "Antony," 26.4.

[4] Page 53—The former president of the Shakespeare Association of America, Maurice Charney, is the one who points out that Shakespeare often makes Cleopatra seem "faintly ridiculous." Charney, *All of Shakespeare,* p. 291.

[5] Page 54—Romans considered pearls so precious and rare they often went in search of them while invading territories. Suetonius even claimed that Caesar invaded Britain partly "in the hope of finding pearls. . . ." Suetonius, *The Lives of the Twelve Caesars,* "Julius Caesar," 47.1.

[6] Page 54—The legend of Cleopatra drinking the dissolved pearls came from Pliny the Elder, a Roman scholar and naturalist. He described Cleopatra's pearls as the "largest that had been ever seen in the whole world. . . ." Pliny the Elder, Book IX, Chapter 58.

[7] Page 56—Cleopatra, as all the Ptolemies, identified with her Greek heritage and her family's connection with Alexander the Great. When historians refer to Egyptians, they often mean the larger Egyptian culture, which sometimes differed from the Greco (Ptolemaic)-Egyptian culture of Cleopatra and the Alexandrians.

[8] Page 56—The native Egyptians, according to White, were a "remarkably superstitious race, and the jewels that swayed and clinked on their necks and wrists served a magical as well as aesthetic purpose. … [In the form of amulets] they could also prevent sickness and ward off the evil eye." White, *Everyday Life in Ancient Egypt,* p. 91.

[9] Page 57—Cleopatra not only flattered Antony, but she also matched his playful personality. Plutarch claimed that the queen "played dice with [Antony], drank with him, and hunted with him. . . ." She also joined in on his pranks. Plutarch, *Makers of Rome,* "Antony," 29.5, p. 296.

[10] Page 57—Plutarch called Antony's attempt to outfox Cleopatra with the fish he never caught one of his many "boyish extravagances." Plutarch, *Makers of Rome,* "Antony," 30.1.

[11] Page 58—Antony and Cleopatra were hashing out a "Client Kingdom" arrangement in which a monarch loyal to him would stay in power. This plan was a more cooperative model than the one in which Roman governors took ownership of the regions. Jones, *Cleopatra,* p. 82.

[12] Page 59—Lucan, a Roman poet, is the one who called Cleopatra a "fatal beauty." He also wrote that she decked herself out with gems and gold and possibly (depending on the translation) wore a see-through dress at a banquet entertaining Caesar. Lucan, *Civil War*, 10.163.

[13] Page 59—Popular movies such as *The Mummy* make it seem as if the *Book of the Dead* is an actual "book." It is not. It's a title Egyptologists use to mean "the great collection of funerary texts which the ancient Egyptian scribes composed for the benefit of the dead." Consisting of "spells and incantations, hymns and litanies, magical formulae and names, words of power and prayers," these so-called books were actually scrolls of papyri often tucked into the coffin of the deceased and painted on the outside of coffins. Budge, *Book of the Dead,* Preface.

[14] Page 60—According to Fletcher in *Egypt Revealed* magazine, "Recent discoveries show hair extensions and dyes were used in Egypt at least as early as 3400 BC." Fall 2000, p. 38.

Chapter Six

[1] Page 62—Modern scholars don't agree that Cleopatra "sapped Antony's will to fight." "Quite the contrary, she missed no opportunity to rouse his ambition and his will to conquer. . . ." Chauveu, *Cleopatra Beyond the Myth,* p. 46.

[2] Page 63—Antony's brother, Lucius Antonius, joined Fulvia in her attempt to overthrow Octavian. Fulvia died, but Octavian forgave Lucius for the attempted coup. Jones, *Cleopatra,* p. 78.

[3] Page 65—Suggesting that a man who was driven by, or even listened to the counsel of his wife, was an insult in ancient Rome. Cicero made these claims against Antony in his "Oration Against Marcus Antonius," also known as *The Sixth Phillippics,* 6.4.

Chapter Seven

[1] Page 68—Grant claims that once Cleopatra's association with Antony was renewed, "she succeeded in driving a much harder bargain." *Cleopatra,* p. 135. Why did he agree so readily to expanding Egypt's lands? Because Antony "needed her resources even more than before." Grant, p. 134.

[2] Page 69—Antony kept Judea in Herod's hands, which likely frustrated Cleopatra. She wanted the region because her ancestors had once owned it. But Antony wanted to "take advantage of the favors Herod owed him," which meant leaving him in charge of Judea. Jones, *Cleopatra,* p. 83.

[3] Page 69—Egypt's territorial history waxes and wanes depending on who was in charge. Did Cleopatra want to go back to the "glory days" of Egypt—one thousand years before her rule—when Ramses II stretched Egypt's holdings into Africa and deep into the Middle East? No; more likely, she wanted to regain the territories her own ancestors—the Ptolemies—had lost over the centuries in skirmishes and wars with other descendants of Alexander the Great's generals (the Seleucids). Syria in particular bounced between the Ptolemies and Seleucids more frantically than a Ping-Pong ball on caffeine.

[4] Page 71—Was Cleopatra faithful to Antony in other ways too? Ancient Jewish historian Josephus claimed that Cleopatra threw herself at Herod. *The Works of Flavius Josephus: Antiquities of the Jews*, Book 15, 4.2. But Cleopatra and Herod were bitter enemies. The claim that Cleopatra tried to seduce her enemy—"was evidently drawn from the personal memoirs of the Jewish king, reeks too much of self-justification for us to accord it credulity," says Chauveau. *Cleopatra: Beyond the Myth*, p. 58. Tyldesley adds, "No other historian tells this tale, which is, to say the least, highly unlikely." *Cleopatra: The Last Queen of Egypt*, p. 167.

[5] Page 72—According to Arab scholar El-Daly, Cleopatra was seen as a "strong and able monarch who was very protective of Egypt." *Egyptology: the Missing Millennium*, p. 131.

[6] Page 72—John, bishop of Nikiu, in his seventh-century work, described Cleopatra as a national heroine and praised her for her wisdom and devotion to her people. Jones, *Cleopatra*, pp. 98–99.

[7] Page 72—El-Daly reiterates that medieval Arab sources represented Cleopatra "as a philosopher and scholar without reference to her physical attributes. But this may also be seen as a reflection of the medieval Arab cultural environment which viewed powerful, intellectual women as normal. ..." *Egyptology: The Missing Millennium*, p. 142.

Chapter Eight

[1] Page 75—Antony was so enraged at the loss, he punished his troops by "decimating" them, which meant his men were divided into groups of ten and one man out of ten—chosen by chance—was killed by his own officers. Plutarch, *Makers of Rome,* "Antony," 39.52, pp. 307–308.

[2] Page 75—Antony had expected to plunder in Parthia after his victories in order to pay his men. He was seriously cash-strapped when he called for help from Cleopatra. Plutarch claimed that "when she was slow in coming, he became distraught and soon gave himself up to heavy drinking. . . ." *Makers of Rome,* "Antony," 51.6, p. 318.

[3] Page 76—Plutarch claimed Cleopatra played all kinds of seductive tricks to keep Antony from seeing Octavia and reconciling with her. *Makers of Rome,* "Antony," 53.52, p. 320.

[4] Page 77—According to Balsdon, "Given good winds, a ship in normal conditions might make a hundred and twenty-sea-miles in a day and if conditions were good, travel by sea was generally far faster than by land." He also says the grain ships from Alexandria to the Roman port in Puteoli took about twelve days in good conditions. But that did not include the land journey to get to the port, and from the port to Rome. *Life and Leisure in Ancient Rome,* p. 226.

[5] Page 76—If Antony had gone back to Octavia, it was as good as saying he couldn't do his job without her brother in charge. No way Antony would've accepted being number two. He'd made his gamble. He had no choice but to renounce his Roman wife if he wanted to rule. Chaveu, *Cleopatra Beyond the Myth,* pp 55–57.

[6] Page 78—In a Roman triumph, the general was celebrated as a victor and hero. He rode in a lavishly decorated chariot, and according to one ancient writer, had his

face and hands painted red and was accompanied by a slave behind him whispering in his ear, "Look behind thee; remember thou art but a man," and not a god. Tertullian, *Apologetic and Practical Treatises,* Vol. I, Chap. 33.

[7] Page 79—A Roman through and through, Antony must have known how his countrymen would respond to his triumph in Egypt. Or perhaps, some wonder, had he really lost touch with how the people of Rome would react to such a move? Either way, it's likely that he thought it was a temporary situation he could ride out until he won more victories in Parthia.

Chapter Nine

[1] Page 81—Plutarch claimed Octavian passed a decree declaring war on Cleopatra and depriving Antony of "authority" because of his association/partnership with the queen. He even claimed that Antony was "no longer responsible for his actions. . . ." It was all *her* fault! *Makers of Rome,* "Antony," 60.4, p. 326. Tyldesley also points out that Octavian's charges against Cleopatra were "remarkably vague"—especially in light of the fact that Cleopatra had proven herself a "faithful Roman vassal" for decades, "supplying assistance to Pompey in 49; preparing a fleet for Antony and Octavian in 42…and Antioch" (for Antony's attack on Parthia). *Cleopatra: Last Queen of Egypt,* p. 175.

[2] Page 82—Octavia took her children (three by her first husband, two by Antony) as well as Antony's sons and reared them in her own home. This made Antony look really, really bad because it seemed as if he were abandoning not just his Roman wife, but his Roman children as well. Also, she raised them all in her own home, not in Octavian's, proving that she could take care of herself. Octavia, a strong woman in her own right, reared strong daughters who played major roles in the politics of the early empire.

[3] Page 81—Tyldesley explains, "Octavian had realized that his troops would agree to fight a foreign enemy, but would not fight Antony, who was still, despite all the negative propaganda, a popular figure." *Cleopatra: Last Queen of Egypt,* p. 175.

[4] Page 80—Plutarch wrote, Antony "abandoned and betrayed the men who were fighting and dying for his cause." *Makers of Rome,* "Antony," 66.35 p.332.

[5] Page 83—According to Chauveau, "Octavian's emissaries succeeded in persuading [Antony's land] soldiers and low-ranking officers…to give up the cause of a leader who seemed to have abandoned them." *Cleopatra: Beyond the Myth,* p. 70.

Chapter Ten

[1] Page 87—Plutarch wrote that she sought to escape from Egypt with "a large sum of money and a strong escort" [a large force] and settle "beyond the frontiers of Egypt." *Makers of Rome,* "Mark Antony," 69.4, p.335. By the Red Sea, he meant the Persian Gulf (sometimes called the Arabian Gulf). She wasn't ready to give up yet!

[2] Page 88—Plutarch said Herod took "a number of legions and cohorts" with him when he defected to Octavian. *Makers of Rome,* "Mark Antony," 71.1. Herod's defection was likely a big blow to Antony, who had handpicked Herod as king of Judea years before and protected much of his kingdom from Cleopatra's expansionistic

plans. Cleopatra, for her part, never trusted Herod. She swore that he would betray Antony one day, and she was right. Jones, *Cleopatra,* p. 122.

[3] Page 88—Plutarch claimed their friends joined this "Order" on "the understanding that they would end their lives together. . . ." *Makers of Rome,* "Antony," 71.3.

[4] Page 88—It took almost a whole year for Octavian to reach Alexandria. Why? First, he had to win over Antony's allies in the East, ensuring their loyalty. Then the seas "closed" for the winter because rough weather made sailing too risky. Plutarch claims it was while they waited for Octavian that Antony and Cleopatra began "partying" hard again. *Makers of Rome,* "Antony," 71.4.

[5] Page 88—Dio claimed that Octavian sent Cleopatra a secret message: "If she would kill Antony, he would grant her pardon" and let her continue ruling. She, of course, did no such thing. Dio, *Roman History,* 51.6.

[6] Page 89—Plutarch wrote that Cleopatra sent a messenger to tell Antony that she was dead, implying that she tricked him into committing suicide. However, given the chaos that likely ensued during the invasion, that may be more propaganda to make the queen look bad. *Makers of Rome,* "Antony," 76.15.

[7] Page 91—Cleopatra, according to Plutarch, was so anguished at the sight of the dying Antony that she smeared her face with his blood and beat at her chest so fiercely, she later got sick from the injuries. *Makers of Rome,* "Antony," 77.16. This did not seem like the reaction of a woman who had "tricked" her husband into killing himself as Plutarch implies.

[8] Page 92—Octavian wanted her alive because he needed her treasure to pay all his soldiers, many of whom were very unhappy about fighting a beloved Roman. Lots of gold, Octavian figured, would soothe their guilt. Plutarch, *Makers of Rome,* "Antony,", 78.16.

[9] Page 92—Refusing food, Plutarch claims, was Cleopatra's way of "releasing" herself from living. Plutarch, *Makers of Rome,* "Antony," 82.3.

[10] Page 92—Plutarch says Octavian "began to frighten her by uttering threats about the fate of her children," and that he applied these threats like "a general uses siege engines." It was the desire to keep her children safe that kept her alive. Plutarch, *Makers of Rome,* "Antony," 82.5.

[11] Page 93—Plutarch also said that the snake may have been brought to her in a water jar or pitcher and that she provoked the snake with a golden pin. *Makers of Rome,* "Antony," 86.2.

[12] Page 93—The servant—one of two—was named Charmian. What the soldier asked was this: "Charmian, is this well done?"—meaning, "Is she really dead?" Plutarch, *Makers of Rome,* "Antony," 85.27.

Chapter Eleven

[1] Page 98.—Octavian also arranged for the murder of Antony's son—the child he had with his third wife, Fulvia—the teenage Antonius. Plutarch, *Makers of Rome,* "Antony," 81.1, p. 344.

[2] Page 98—Roller writes that Cleopatra's two surviving boys, Alexander Helios and Ptolemy Philadelphus, likely "died naturally" in Rome after participating in Octavian's triumph celebrating the defeat of their parents. He conjectures that Ptolemy Philadelphus died first and that Alexander Helios died "before military and marriageable age." *The World of Juba II and Kleopatra Selene,* p. 84.

[3] Page 99—It was the Roman writer Suetonius who claimed Caligula had Cleopatra's grandson killed because of his coat. *Lives of Twelve Caesars,* "Caligula," 35.2.

[4] Page 100—Tyldesley says Octavian "claimed Egypt as his own personal estate." Then he put the "relatively lowly Cornelius Gallus, a prefect of the equestrian rank" in charge. Any Roman who wanted to visit Egypt needed "permission from Octavian." He was also "unconcerned about offending local priests, he refused to visit the Apis bull, announcing…that he worshipped gods, not cattle." So much for religious tolerance and respect! *Cleopatra: Last Queen of Egypt,* p. 203. Chauveau agrees that Octavian chose weak men to manage Egypt as a form of self-protection, fearing that "Egypt's riches could serve the interests of some politician who might compete with him for the empire…" *Egypt in the Age of Cleopatra,* p. 191.

[5] Page 101—One prominent historian wrote, "There is . . . serious danger that we might end up falling for Octavian's presentation" of events. "All of this is myth which Octavian, once victorious, had a long time to create and refashion. We should . . . construct for ourselves a more skeptical view" of his story. *Cleopatra of Egypt: From History to Myth,* p. 193.

[6] Page 102—Octavian seized Antony's will from the house of the Vestal Virgins— breaking a sacred law that no one called him on. Tyldesley says he then "read what he *claimed* [emphasis mine] to be extracts from Antony's will." *Cleopatra: Last Queen of Egypt.* p. 172. Jones writes, "Whether Octavian accurately represented the contents of Antony's will, or if Antony even deposited a will in the Temple of Vesta, is not known." *Cleopatra, Last Queen of Egypt,* p. 102.

[7] Page 102—One scholar comments: "The fact that the queen's death provoked such financial sacrifice shows us just how much she was venerated." *Cleopatra of Egypt : From History to Myth,* p. 140.

[8] Page 103—Octavian's propaganda has influenced our view of Cleopatra since her defeat. However, finds such as this humble weaving reflect the love she had for her land. Chaveau writes of the weaving: "Such was the memory [of the queen] that the Egyptian people…piously prepared to preserve of the last and greatest of their queens." *Cleopatra: Beyond the Myth,* p. 80.

Timeline

BCE (Before the Common Era)

323—Ptolemy I, a Greek Macedonian, takes over Egypt after Alexander the Great's death. The era of Greek rule begins.

69—Cleopatra is born.

51—Cleopatra's father, Ptolemy XII, "Auletes" dies, leaving Cleopatra VII and her little brother in charge of Egypt.

48—Cleopatra kicked out of Alexandria when little brother's advisers take over on his behalf. Cleopatra raises an army. Julius Caesar arrives in Alexandria. Pompey beheaded. Cleopatra sneaks in, snug-in-a-rug, to meet Caesar. He restores Cleopatra to her throne.

47—Caesarion (Ptolemy Caesar), son of Cleopatra and Julius Caesar, is born.

44—Julius Caesar is assassinated.

43—Antony, Octavian, and Lepidus form a triumvirate.

41—Antony calls Cleopatra to Tarsus; follows her to Alexandria.

40—Antony returns to Rome and marries Octavian's sister, Octavia. Cleopatra gives birth to twins, Alexander Helios and Cleopatra Selene.

37—Antony leaves Octavia; calls Cleopatra to him in Antioch.

36—Antony is defeated in Parthia; Cleopatra gives birth to Ptolemy Philadelphus, their third child.

34—Antony holds Donations of Alexandria, giving Roman territory to Cleopatra and their children.

32—Antony divorces Octavian's sister. Octavian declares war on Cleopatra.

31—Antony and Cleopatra escape from Actium. Almost all of Antony's forces defect to Octavian's side. Cleopatra and Antony return to Alexandria.

30—Antony falls on his sword. Octavian has Caesarion killed. Cleopatra commits suicide, ending the era of Greek rule. Cleopatra's children sent to live in Rome. Octavian annexes Egypt, treating it as his personal property. The era of Roman rule begins.

25—Cleopatra Selene, daughter of Cleopatra VII and Mark Antony, marries Juba II in Mauretania (today's Morocco and Algeria).

1—Ptolemy of Mauretania, son of Cleopatra Selene and Juba II and grandson of Cleopatra and Antony, is born.

CE (Common Era)

6—Cleopatra Selene dies.

14—Octavian, renamed Augustus, dies at seventy-seven. He ruled Rome for forty-four years.

40—Ptolemy of Mauretania, Cleopatra's grandson and Cleopatra Selene's son, is murdered by Emperor Caligula, who envied his pretty cloak and executed him. The irony? Caligula was the grandson of Antonia the Younger, half sister to Cleopatra Selene. The last of the Ptolemies, then, was murdered by his own second cousin.

Glossary

A

Actium—A promontory off the coast of Greece where Octavian and his forces blocked Antony's forces. Antony and Cleopatra escaped, but all of Antony's men defected to Octavian's side.

Alexander the Great—Macedonian Greek warrior king who conquered most of what today we call the Middle East. He took Egypt from the Persians (Iraq-Iran) in 332 BCE, beginning the era of Greek rule in Egypt.

Alexandria—City founded by Alexander the Great in 331 BCE. Became the political, commercial, and educational center of Egypt under the rule of the Ptolemies.

Alexandrian War—Civil war between Cleopatra and her younger brother and sister, who aimed to usurp her power. Julius Caesar, though vastly outnumbered, defeated the Egyptian forces and reinstated Cleopatra as ruler of Egypt.

Anubis—Jackal-headed Egyptian god of embalming.

Apis bull—A bull considered sacred in ancient Egypt. Originally seen as the incarnation of the creator god Ptah, it later became widely known as the incarnation of the god Osiris, Lord of Death.

Arsinoe—Cleopatra's younger sister. She began the Alexandrian War after proclaiming herself pharaoh. Julius Caesar defeated her and her forces. He marched her in his triumph.

Asp—Egyptian cobra, the type of snake Cleopatra used, according to legend.

Augustus—Meaning "Revered One," a name Octavian took for himself after emerging as the sole ruler and first emperor of Rome.

Auletes—Greek nickname meaning "Piper"; Cleopatra's father.

B

BCE—The abbreviation for Before the Common Era, which is the secular (non-religious) replacement for BC (Before Christ) used by historians worldwide.

Book of the Dead—Funerary text made up of individualized prayers, hymns, chants, and spells designed to ensure the deceased's passage into the afterworld.

Buchis bull—A sacred bull, the Buchis was the representation of the gods Ra and Osiris, though sometimes linked with the war god Montu.

C

Caesar—Also known as Julius Caesar. Julius Caesar adopted Octavian in his will, after which Octavian took his name. From then on, all Roman emperors called themselves Caesar.

Caesarion—"Little Caesar"; the nickname for the child born of Cleopatra and Julius Caesar in 47 BCE.

CE—The abbreviation for common era, the most widely used system for numbering years. Replaced AD (Anno Domini).

Cicero—Roman lawyer, writer, and statesman. Famous for his speeches, he was a strong supporter of a republican government and disliked both Julius Caesar and Mark Antony, as well as Cleopatra.

Civil War—Armed conflict between opposing groups within the same country. Octavian's fight with Antony was a civil war, though he presented it as a war against Cleopatra.

D

Defect (verb)—To abandon allegiance to a cause or person. In Antony's case, most of his forces defected from his side to Octavian's, effectively killing his chances against Octavian.

Demotic—A later form of the ancient Egyptian language; a script in use during the later reign of the Greek Ptolemies. One of the languages written on the Rosetta Stone, used to decipher hieroglyphics.

E

East, the—The ancient Greeks and Romans called everything east of Rome "the East." From Turkey, down to Egypt, and past Arabia, Romans often considered "the East" corrupt and dangerous. Octavian used those prejudices to smear Cleopatra as a danger to Rome.

F

Feather of Truth—In ancient Egyptian religious belief, a person's heart was weighed against the Feather of Truth, or the principles of *ma'at* (order, truth). If the heart weighed as much as or less than the Feather of Truth, the deceased could continue to eternal life in the afterworld. In Egyptian art, the Feather of Truth is often depicted as an ostrich feather or, sometimes, a peacock feather.

H

Hieroglyphics/hieroglyphs—A form of picture writing used by the ancient Egyptians, comprised of more than two thousand characters. A rebus or picture puzzle is a modern type of hieroglyphic writing.

I

Isis—Egyptian mother goddess; the wife of her brother, Osiris, and mother of Horus. Isis worship became one of the most powerful religions of the ancient world. Cleopatra associated herself with Isis.

J

Julian calendar—The twelve-month solar calendar Julius Caesar introduced to Rome after spending time in Egypt with Cleopatra and her court of astronomers. Although the calendar had been in use in Egypt for thousands of years, Julius Caesar took credit for "inventing" it.

K

Kohl—Black eyeliner makeup used to darken the rims of eyes and eyebrows in ancient Egypt. Both men and women painted their eyes with kohl.

L

Library of Alexandria, or Great Library of Alexandria—The royal library of ancient Alexandria, begun by Cleopatra's ancestors Ptolemy I and Ptolemy II. It was said to hold the largest collection of works in the ancient world. The library also contained a famous learning center and museum.

Lighthouse of Alexandria—One of the Seven Wonders of the Ancient World, the Lighthouse at Alexandria was begun by Cleopatra's ancestor Ptolemy I. A three-story building reaching up to four hundred feet, the lighthouse featured a giant polished bronze mirror to reflect an ever-burning fire at its tip. According to legend, the fire could be seen from several miles away.

Lower Egypt/Upper Egypt—Ancient Egypt was divided into two regions—Upper and Lower Egypt. Geographically, even though Alexandria was at Egypt's northernmost tip, it was considered Lower Egypt, while Upper Egypt included what we think of as the southern half of Egypt. The two kingdoms of Upper and Lower Egypt united in 3000 BCE. Pharaohs were known as the rulers of the Two Lands and wore double crowns to signify both regions.

M

Ma'at—The ancient Egyptian concept of truth, order, balance, law, morality, and justice. Ma'at was sometimes personified as a goddess. In the weighing-of-the-heart ceremony, the Feather of Truth represented ma'at.

Mausoleum—A large, often elaborately decorated tomb.

Mummy—The body of a person or an animal that has been embalmed and wrapped. In ancient Egypt, people believed the soul left the body upon death, but that it would be reunited with its body in the afterlife if the body had been properly preserved.

O

Octavian—*see* Augustus

Osiris—The ancient Egyptian god of the underworld and the dead. Also, the husband of Isis and father of Horus.

P

Parthia—In the ancient world, what is now commonly known as the region of Iran, Iraq, Syria, Armenia, Turkey, and other Middle Eastern states. A strong empire that often challenged Rome for territory and supremacy.

Pharaoh—A ruler of ancient Egypt, similar to a king or queen.

Ptolemy—The Macedonian Greek general who took over Egypt after Alexander the Great's death. He and his family ruled Egypt for 250 years. Cleopatra was the last of the Ptolemaic rulers.

R

Republic—A political system or form of government in which citizens elect representatives to govern for them. Ancient Rome prided itself on having a republic form of government, which ended for good when Octavian defeated Mark Antony.

S

Scroll—A roll of papyrus or other form of paper used for writing. Books in the ancient world were actually a series of scrolls.

T

Tiber—The third-longest river in Italy. In ancient times, Rome was on the Tiber's eastern banks though today it extends all the way to the western seacoast. When Cleopatra visited Rome with Julius Caesar, she stayed in a villa across the Tiber from Rome, because as a monarch she was not allowed into the city itself.

Toga—An outer garment worn by Roman citizens, often draped over a tunic.

Tomb—A crypt or vault for burying the dead. In ancient Egypt, tombs were often hidden underground to prevent looting. Cleopatra's tomb has not been found.

Triumvirate—A group of three men who shared governing and military power in ancient Rome.

U

Usurp—To take or seize without permission; used when referring to power or control.

V

Venus—The goddess of love in Roman religion. In the Greek religion, she was known as Aphrodite.

Bibliography

(Links active at time of publication)

Primary Sources

Book of the Dead: The Hieroglyphic Transcript of the Papyrus of Ani. Translated by E. A. Wallis Budge. Whitefish MT: Kessinger, 2003.

Caesar, Julius, *The Civil War.* Translated by Jane Gardner. London: Penguin Classics. 1967.

Cicero, Marcus Tullius. *Letters of Marcus Tullius Cicero.* New York: Collier & Son, 1909. Harvard Classics, Internet Ancient History Sourcebook. Also, *Orations: The fourteen orations against Marcus Antonius (Philippics),* translation CD Yonge (1903);
http://www.perseus.tufts.edu/cgi-bin/ptext?lookup=Cic.+Phil.+6.4

Dio, Cassius. *Roman History.* Loeb Classical Library Edition, Vol. 7. 1917. Public domain access:
http://penelope.uchicago.edu/Thayer/E/Roman/Texts/Cassius_Dio/51*.html

Herodotus. *The Histories.* Translated by Aubrey de Selincourt. New York: Penguin, 1996.

Josephus, Flavius. *The Works of Flavius Josephus, Antiquities of the Jews.* Translated by William Whiston. Thompson and Thomas. Chicago: 1901.

Lucan (Marcus Anneus Lucanus). *Civil War.* Book X, "Caesar in Egypt".

London: Loeb Classics Library, 1928. The Online Medieval and Classical Library.
http://omacl.org/Pharsalia/book10.html.

Pliny the Elder. *The Natural History,* Book IX. Translated by J. Bostock. London: Taylor and Francis, 1855.
http://www.perseus.tufts.edu/cgi-bin/ptext?lookup=Plin.+Nat.+9.58

Plutarch. *Makers of Rome: Nine Lives.* "Marc Antony." Translated by Ian Scott-Kilvert. Baltimore: Penguin, 1965.

———. *Fall of the Roman Republic: Six Lives.* "Pompey" and "Caesar." Translated by Rex Warner. Baltimore: Penguin Classics, 1959.

Suetonius. The *Lives of the Twelve Caesars.* Translated by H. M. Bird. Chicago: Argus, 1930.

Tacitus, Cornelius. *The Annals of Imperial Rome.* Translated by Michael Grant. Hammondsworth, England: Penguin, 1973.

Tertullian. *Apologetic and Practical Treatises.* Translated by C. Dodgson. www.tertullian.org.

Secondary Sources

Balsdon, J. P .V. D. *Life and Leisure in Ancient Rome.* London: Phoenix Press. 2002.

Bradford, Ernle. *Cleopatra.* New York: Harcourt Brace Jovanovich, 1972.

Charney, Maurice. *All of Shakespeare.* Ithaca: Columbia University Press, 1993.

Chauveau, Michel. *Cleopatra Beyond the Myth.* Ithaca: Cornell University Press, 2002

———. *Egypt in the Age of Cleopatra.* Cornell University Press, 2000

David, A. Rosalie. *Handbook to Life in Ancient Egypt.* New York: Facts on File, 1998.

Dickson, Katrina. Classicist, Emory University. Series of interviews, Spring 2008.

El-Daly, Okasha. *Egyptology: The Missing Millennium: Ancient Egypt in Medieval Arabic Writings.* London: University College London Press, 2005.

Geddes & Grosset. *Ancient Egypt Myth & History.* New Lanark, Scotland: Geddes & Grosset, 1997.

Grant, Michael. *Cleopatra.* Edison, NJ: Castle, 2004.

———. *From Alexander to Cleopatra: The Hellenistic World.* New York: Collier, 1990.

Grant, Neil. *The Egyptians.* New York: Oxford University Press, 1996.

Hamer, Mary. *Signs of Cleopatra: History, Politics, Representation.* New York: Routledge, 1993.

Hart, George. *Egyptian Myths.* Austin: University of Texas Press, 1990.

Hawass, Zahi. *Silent Images: Women in Pharaonic Egypt.* New York: Harry N. Abrams, 2000.

James, Peter, and Nick Thorpe. *Ancient Mysteries.* New York: Ballantine, 1999.

Jones, Prudence, J. *Cleopatra.* London: Haus, 2006.

———. *Cleopatra: A Sourcebook.* Norman: University of Oklahoma Press, 2006.

Kleiner, Diana, E. E. *Cleopatra and Rome.* Cambridge: Belknap Press of Harvard University Press, 2005.

Matyszak, Philip. *The Enemies of Rome: From Hannibal to Attila the Hun.* New York: Thames & Hudson, 2004.

Mooney, William West. *Travel Among the Ancient Romans.* Boston: R.G. Badger, 1920.

Pollard, Justin, and Howard Reid. *The Rise and Fall of Alexandria: Birthplace of the Modern Mind.* New York: Viking, 2006.

Robinson, Andrew. *The Story of Writing.* London: Thames & Hudson, 1995.

Robins, Gay. *Reflections of Women in the New Kingdom.* San Antonio: Van Siclen Books, 1995.

———. *Women in Ancient Egypt.* Cambridge: Harvard University Press, 1993.

Roller, Duane W. *The World of Juba II and Kleopatra Selene: Royal Scholarship on Rome's African Frontier.* New York: Routledge, 2003.

Shakespeare, William. *Antony and Cleopatra.* New York: Washington Square Press, 1999.

———. *Julius Caesar.* New York: Washington Square Press, 1992.

Shaw, George Bernard. *Caesar and Cleopatra.* New York: Brentano's, 1906.

Tames, Richard. *Ancient Egyptian Children.* Oxford: Heinemann Library, 2002.
Tyldesley, Joyce. *Cleopatra: Last Queen of Egypt.* New York: Basic Books, 2008.
————. *The Mummy.* London: Carlton Books, 1999.
Versluis, Arthur. *The Egyptian Mysteries.* New York: Arkana, 1988.
Walker, Susan, and Peter Higgs, (eds). *Cleopatra of Egypt: From History to Myth.* London: British Museum Press, 2005.
————, and Sally Ann Ashton. *Cleopatra; Ancients in Action.* London: Bristol Classical Press, 2006.
White, Jon Manchip. *Everyday Life in Ancient Egypt.* Mineola,NY: Dover, 2002.

Articles

Fletcher, Joann. "Strange Tales of Egyptian Hair." *Egypt Revealed.* Fall 2000.
Jones, Prudence. "Cleopatra's Cocktail." *Classical World.* 103.2, 2010.
Lawler, Andrew. "Wonders of Alexandria: Rediscovering the Fabled City of Cleopatra." *Smithsonian* (April 2007).
Pinkowski, Jennifer. "Egypt's Ageless Goddess." *Archaeology* (September/October, 2006).
Ross, Kelley, L., "Hellenistic Monarchs Down to the Roman Empire." 2008. www.friesian.com/hist-1.htm
Tyldesley, Joyce, "Marriage and Motherhood in Ancient Egypt." *History Today* (April 1994).

Picture Sources

(Links active at time of publication)

Cover
Photograph copyright © Elizabeth Salib (www.elizabethsalib.com)

Sidebar backgrounds
All Gizah Pyramids. © Ricardo Liberto, Wikimedia Commons/Creative Commons.

Tab backgrounds
Temple of Kalabsha in Egyptian Nubia. Roman era. © Lassi, Wikimedia Commons/Creative Commons.

Title page
Augustus, Cleopatra's conqueror, shown as Pharaoh on Temple of Kalabsha in Egyptian Nubia. Roman era. © Lassi, Wikimedia Commons/Creative Commons.

Introduction
6. Playing Senet from the tomb of Nefertari. Photo: The Yorck Project, Wikimedia Commons/public domain.
7. Lillie Langtry, actress (1853-1929), as Cleopatra. Library of Congress.
8. Playing Senet from the tomb of Nefertari. Photo: The Yorck Project, Wikimedia Commons/public domain.

Chapter One
9: Cleopatra VII. 1st Century BCE. Capitoline Museum, Rome. © Archaeology Images.
11: Map of Ancient Egypt. Courtesy of public domain images at Karen Whimsy: http://karenswhimsy.com/public-domain-images.
12: Ptolemy XII Auletes. Marble, First century BC, from Egypt. Louvre Museum, Paris. Photo: Jastrow, Wikimedia Commons/public domain.
13: Taxpayer in scribe's office. from *History of Egypt, Chaldea, Syria, Babylonia, and Assyria in Light of Recent Discovery.* by G. Maspero. London: The Grolier Society, 1903-1906. Project Gutenberg, public domain.
14: Plutarch. Archaeological Museum, Delphi, Greece. Photo: Tiu Fralli, Wikimedia Commons/public domain.
15: Homer. Bust of Homer, British Museum, London. Wikimedia Commons/public domain.
16: Alexander the Great. Courtesy of the Michael C. Carlos Museum of Emory University.
17: Egyptian war god, Montu. Karnak relief. © Steve F-E-Cameron. Wikimedia Commons/Creative Commons.
18: Mummified head of an Apis Bull. © Mary Harrsch. Photographed at the Rosicrucian Egyptian Museum, San Jose, California.

19: Papyrus with declaration of tax exemption of the Roman citizen Q. Cascellius, probably bearing Queen Cleopatra VII's signature sign-off ("Genestho"), dated to 33 BCE. Aegyptisches Museum, Staatiche Museen zu Berlin, Berlin. © Archaeology Images. Photo by Margrete Buesing.
20: Golden pendant bearing the name Osorkon II. 22nd Dynasty. Louvre Museum, Paris. © Jon Bodsworth, Egypt Archive.

Chapter Two
22: Bust of Julius Caesar. National Archaeological Museum of Naples. Photo: Andreas Wahra, Wikimedia Commons/public domain.
23: Pompey the Great. Carlsberg Glyptotek, Copenhagan. Photo: Gunnar Bach Pedersen, Wikimedia Commons/public domain.
24: Pompey Coin. CNG coins (http:www.cngcoins.com). Wikimedia Commons/Creative Commons.
26: Statue of Queen Cleopatra VII. Basalt, second half of the first century BCE. Hermitage, St. Petersburg, Russia. © George Shuklin, Wikimedia Commons/Creative Commons.
27: Bust of Julius Caesar. Altes Museum, Berlin. Photo: Louis le Grand, Wikimedia Commons/ public domain.
29: Statue of Caesar. Commissioned in 1696 for the Gardens of Versilles. From the Gardens of the Tuileries, 1872. Department of Sculptures, Louvre Museum, Paris. Photo: Jastrow, Wikimedia Commons/public domain.
30: Ship on the Nile. From *History of Egypt, Chaldea, Syria, Babylonia, and Assyria in Light of Recent Discovery*. by G. Maspero. London: The Grolier Society, 1903-1906. Project Gutenberg, public domain.

Chapter Three
31:. Relief of Ptolemy XII Auletes, from the temple at Kom Ombo. Photo: Crucifixion, Wikimedia Commons/public domain.
32: Bay of Alexandria . Copyright © Ziad Nour. www.perankhgroup.com.
34: Early second century scroll discovered near Oxyrhynchus, Egpyt. Sackler Library, Oxford. Photo: Apollodorus, Wikimedia Commons/public domain.
35 (top) The Celsius Library, Ephesus, Turkey. Photo: Djenan Kozic, Wikimedia Commnos/ public domain.
35 (bottom) Modern Library of Alexandria. Photo: Redturtle, Wikimedia Commons/public domain.
37: Valley of Kings as seen from the Nile. © Alchemica. Wikimedia Commons/Creative Commons.
38: Isis painting in the tomb of Seti I, Valley of the Kings. Yorck Project Wikimedia Commons/ public domain.
39: The Lighthouse of Alexandria. © Kenn Brown, Mondolithic Studios.
40: Egyptian Astronomy. © NebMaatRa. Wikimedia Commons/GNU General Public License.

Chapter Four
41: Birth of the god Harpare in the Temple of Armant, built by Cleopatra VII to honor the birth of Caesarion. Drawing by Karl Richard Lepsius (1810-1884). Wikimedia Commons/public domain.
42: Calpurnia from *Promptuari Iconum Insigniorum*, 1553. Wikimedia Commons/public domain.
43: (top): Fresco from the Villa of P. Fannio Sinistore in Boscoreale, now located at the Metropolitan Museum of Art, New York City. Wikimedia Commons/public domain.
43: (bottom): *Assassination of Caesar* by Jean-Léon Gérôme (1824-1904). Oil on canvas. Walters Art Gallery, Baltimore, Maryland.Wikimedia Commons/public domain.

44: (top): Ancient Egyptian toy cat. Copyright © Mary Harrsch.

44: Ptolemaic boy juggling balls. CSU Image Project, School of Art and Design, San Jose State University. Copyright © Kathleen Cohen.

44 (bottom): Playing Senet from the tomb of Nefertari. Photo: The Yorck Project, Wikimedia Commons/public domain.

45: *Cleopatra* by John William Waterhouse (1849-1917). Wikimedia Commnos/public domain.

46: Bust of Cicero. Scanned from a book dated 1900. "Photogravure from the marble bust in the Prado Gallery at Madrid." Presumably in Madrid's Musuem of Aarchaeology. Wikimedia Commons/public domain.

47: Head of Octavian/Augustus. Bronze 27-25 BCE. British Museum, London.
© Steve F-E-Cameron, Wikimedia Commons/Creative Commons.

48: Augustus shown as Pharaoh on Temple of Kalabsha in Egyptian Nubia. Roman era.
© Lassi, Wikimedia Commons/Creative Commons.

Chapter Five

49: Marcus Antonius/Mark Antony: From *A Smaller History of Rome* by William Smith, Abel Hendy Jones Greenidge, Andrew Di. Wikimedia Commons/public domain.

51: Boat on Nile. From *History of Egypt, Chaldea, Syria, Babylonia, and Assyria in Light of Recent Discovery*. by G. Maspero. London: The Grolier Society, 1903-1906. Project Gutenberg, public domain.

52: William Shakespeare. Chandos Portrait (1610), perhaps by John Taylor. National Portrait Gallery, London. Wikimedia Commons/public domain.

53: Vivian Leigh as Cleopatra. Tom P. Conroy, Movie Stills Archive.

54: *Antony and Cleopatra* by Lawrence Alma-Tadema (1836-1912). Oil on panel. Wikimedia Commons/public domain.

55: Egyptian banquet/music. Courtesy of public domain images at Karen Whimsy: http://karenswhimsy.com/public-domain-images.

56: Gold pendant with Udjat eye above a scarab with Horus wings. Photo copyright
© Jon Bodsworth, Egypt Archive.

57: Antony side of Antony/Octavian Aureus coin. 41 BCE.CNG coins (http:www.cngcoins. com). Wikimedia Commons/Creative Commons.

58: Limestone stele of Cleopatra VII dressed as pharaoh presenting offerings to Isis, 51 BCE. Louvre Museum, Paris. Photo: Jastrow, Wikimedia Commons/public domain.

59: Cosmetics spoon of Swimming Woman with Duck. Louvre Museum, Paris.
© Rama.Wikimedia Commons/Creative Commons.

60: (left) Lapis Lazuli wig. British Museum, London. Copyright © Jon Bodsworth, Egypt Archive. (right) Double-wig: 11th Dynasty. © The British Museum Images.

Chapter Six

61. Octavia Minor. Ara Pacis Museum, Rome. © G.dallorto. Wikimedia Commons/Creative Commons.

62: Coin of Fulvia Antonis. CNG coins (http:www.cngcoins.com). Wikimedia Commons/Creative Commons.

64: Coin of young Cleopatra wearing a broad diadem band. Ascalon, 50-49 BCE. © PHGCOM. British Museum, London. Wikimedia Commons/public domain.

65: Head of a statue of Hercules. Crown of poplar leaves, after a Greek statue (330-320 BC). 1st century CE. Photo: Bibi Saint-Pol, Wikimedia Commons/public domain.

Chapter Seven

66: Painting of a woman, maybe Cleopatra VII. 1ˢᵗ century CE. Naples, National Archaeological Museum. © Archaeological Images.

67: Musician with Harp and Cithara (lyre). Roman fresco from Pompeii. Photo: Wolfgang Rieger. Wikimedia Commons/public domain.

68: Theda Bara in the role of Cleopatra a now lost 1917 film. Wikimedia Commons/public domain.

70: Detail from *Cleopatra and Peasant* (1838) by Eugene Delacroix (1798-1863). Oil on canvas. Ackland Museum, University of North Carolina at Chapel Hill. Wikimedia Commons/public domain.

71. Detail of Cleopatra sculpture. Sculptor: Leonhard Kern (1588-1662). Bode-Musuem, Berlin. Photo: Andreas Praefcke. Wikimedia Commons /public domain.

Chapter Eight

73: Parthian prisoner wearing a Phrygian cap, detail of the so-called Great Cameo of France. Roman, 1st century AD. Cabinet des médailles de laBibliothèque nationale de France. © Marie-Lan Nguyen. Wikimedia Commons/Creative Commons.

74: Map of Parthia 100-50 BCE. © Dbachman.Wikimedia Commons/Creative Commons.

76: Roman warship. Courtesy of public domain images at Karen Whimsy: http://karenswhimsy.com/public-domain-images.

77. Roman Road in Algiers. Photo by PhR61.Wikimedia Commons/Creative Commons.

79: *Roman Triumph of Titus and Vespasian*. Oil on canvas (1537-1540) by Giulio Romano (1499-1546). Wikimedia Commons/public domain.

80: Map: Donations of Alexandria. Map: Howard Wiseman, Wikimedia Commons/Creative Commons.

Chapter Nine

81: *Battle Actium, 2 September 31 BC* by Lorenzo A. Castro, painted in 1672. Wikimedia Commons/public domain.

82. Marcus Vispanius Agrippa. Plaster cast in Pushkin Museum, after bust in Louvre Museum, Paris. © shakko, Wikimedia Commons/Creative Commons.

83. Bronze prow of a ship believed to have sunk at Battle of Actium. © The British Museum Images.

84. (left): Bust of Cleopatra created in her lifetime (1ˢᵗ century BCE). Berlin Museum. Photo: Louis le Grand. Wikimedia Commons/public domain.

84. (right): Sarah Berndhart as Cleopatra. Library of Congress.

85 (top left): Elizabeth Taylor as Cleopatra. Tom P. Conroy, Movie Stills Archive.
(top right): Ruth St. Denis. Library of Congress.Wikimedia Commons/public domain.
(bottom left): Cleopatra recreation, courtesy of Image Foundry Studios, LTD./BBC.
(bottom right): Claudette Colbert. Tom P. Conroy, Movie Stills Archive.

86: Cleopatra VII committing suicide. Claude Bertin. Marble, before 1697. Louvre Museum, Paris. Photo: Jastrow, Wikimedia Commons/public domain.

Chapter Ten

87: Ships on the Nile. From *History of Egypt, Chaldea, Syria, Babylonia, and Assyria in Light of Recent Discovery*. by G. Maspero. London: The Grolier Society, 1903-1906. Project Gutenberg/public domain.

89: Letters of Butehamun. Copyright © Ziad Nour. www.perankhgroup.com.
90: (top) Antony and Cleopatra. Courtesy of public domain images at Karen Whimsy: http://karenswhimsy.com/public-domain-images.
(bottom): Relief of gladiator on funerary stele. Bissing collection/Munich. Photo: Bibi Saint-Pol, Wikimedia Commons/public domain.
91: Tomb of Pashedo at Deirr el-Medina. © karioinfo4u. Wikimedia Commons/Creative Commons.
93: *Death of Cleopatra*. Oil on canvas by Johann Liss (ca. 1597-1631). Wikimedia Commons/ public domain.

Chapter Eleven
94: Poster for film *Cleopatra*, starring Theda Bara, 1917. Wikimedia Commons/public domain.
95: Statue of Cleopatra at Rosicrucian Egyptian Museum, San Jose, California. Photo: E. Michael Smith Chiefio, Wikimedia Commons/public domain.
96: (top) Ptolemaic mummy, courtesy of the Michael C. Carlos Museum of Emory University.
96: (bottom) Drawing of mummification. From *History of Egypt, Chaldea, Syria, Babylonia, and Assyria in Light of Recent Discovery*. by G. Maspero. London: The Grolier Society, 1903-1906. Project Gutenberg, public domain.
97: Close up of Book of the Dead of Hunefer, 19th Dynasty. © Jon Bodsworth. Wikipedia Commons/Creative Commons.
98: Cleopatra and Caesarion, Temple of Denderah. Photo: Rowan, Wikimedia Commons/public domain.
99: (top) Ptolemy II Philadelphus. Brooklyn Museum. © Keith Schengili-Roberts, Wikimedia Commons/Creative Commons.
    (middle) Cleopatra Selene. Copyright © Kathleen Cohen, CSU Image Project, San Jose State University.
    (bottom) Ptolemy of Mauretania. Metropolitan Museum of Art, New York City.
Copyright © Mary Harrsch.
100: Augustus of Prima Porta statue. Museo Chiaramonti, Vatican, Rome. 1st Century.
© Andreas Wahra, Wikimedia Commons/Creative Commons.
102: Head of Hapshetsut, 18th Dynasty. Metropolitan Museum of Art, New York City. © Postdlf. Wikimedia Commons/Creative Commons.
103: Stele with head of Ptolemaic Queen. Courtesy of the Michael C. Carlos Museum of Emory University.

Index

Italicized page numbers refer to pictures.

127